FROM
BIG BOTTOM
TO
BROADWAY

Remembering the
Singing Hilltoppers

DON K. MCGUIRE

ISBN: 978-1-4834-7569-1 (sc)
ISBN: 978-1-4834-7568-4 (e)

Lulu Publishing Services rev. date: 01/03/2018

For all the years of giving me great love and joy
I dedicate this book to my wife, Maxine, to our three children, Cindy,
Kreis and Lisa, nine grandchildren, and two great-grand children.

Special thanks go to my fine editor Janet Wiebke and to my
master computer expert, granddaughter Emily Shell.

CHAPTER ONE

From somewhere in the darkness of the theatre comes a mystery voice announcing that the show is about to begin.

"AND NOW LADIES AND GENTLEMEN, THE CHICAGO THEATRE IS PROUD TO PRESENT THE STARS OF OUR SHOW! THESE FOUR YOUNG MEN HAVE CAPTURED THE HEARTS OF MUSIC LOVERS ALL OVER AMERICA! TOGETHER LET'S GIVE A BIG CHICAGO WELCOME TO JIMMY SACCA, BILLY VAUGHN, SEYMOUR SPIEGELMAN AND DON MCGUIRE, BETTER KNOWN AS AMERICA'S NUMBER ONE VOCAL GROUP. HERE THEY ARE— THE HILLTOPPERS!!"

How in the world did a football player, a licensed barber, a music major, and a college basketball player from the hills of Kentucky get together and become the number one vocal group in America? Was it strictly luck that they reached such stardom or did ole Mr. Fate have something to do with it? How about "lucky fate?" Maybe that will be a good enough tag to put on the foursome.

It wasn't difficult to understand how so many lives were changed simply because an unknown songwriter wrote a pretty love ballad called "Trying". Of the thousands of composers in this country how did Billy Vaughn come to the front and be fortunate enough to write a tune that the music public was ready to buy? Maybe it was because he was an undiscovered music genius and knew secrets only geniuses know. Overrating him? Not a chance. His uncommon talent put words and music together and touched our emotions. We amateur writers can't do that very well.

In April of 1952 four voices and one piano gave life to music and words jotted down on paper. In only a few short weeks the tune "Trying" was being hummed, whistled, and purchased until 750,000 copies were sold.

Only in America!

CHAPTER TWO

Hazard, Kentucky, my hometown in the hills of our state, was named after the great naval hero Oliver Hazard Perry. To my knowledge nobody knows why the name was chosen. I think ol' Oliver would be proud to know that the county (Perry) was also named after him.

Something very important happened to me in Oliver's town in 1931. It was in this community that my Mother tired of carrying me around so I was born and turned loose to enter the world.

Two years earlier she had toted my brother Bobby until she saw fit to release him. His entrance into our home came on a fifty acre piece of flat land known as Big Bottom.

Bobby and I were blessed with parents who had strong value systems. Asher and Pearl McGuire insisted that we use proper grammar, always be courteous and have good manners. They also insisted that we go to Sunday School and church for what seemed to be fifty times each week. We were there more than the janitor.

Our minister believed that his sermons should go for at least one hour. But the invitation to confess your sins at the altar would sometimes take even longer than that. While confession and forgiveness were cleansing souls, David White and I were in the balcony devouring bags of peanuts. When we were discovered eating in church we were pulled by our ears to the altar where we apologized to the Lord.

The penalty for our transgressions was to memorize twenty Bible verses and be able to recite them in front of our entire Sunday School class. I claimed to have laryngitis or some other malady that had taken my speaking voice.

Nobody believed me.

*Church balcony peanut eaters, David White (far right),
with his accomplice (me) next to him*

CHÁPTER THREE

When I look back to my young years I think the memories of my time spent in elementary school are worth keeping alive. My fourth grade teacher should never been allowed to teach. She was a mean woman who would have made a perfect guard at a German concentration camp. Instead she was hired to teach young, innocent children.

A good example of her thoughtless demands was the way students had to correct an error on an assignment written in ink. She made us use a razor blade to scrape away whatever error was made. Once when I reached inside my desk to get a sheet of notebook paper I accidentally ran my finger onto the sharp edge of my blade, bringing blood. I was afraid to tell her what I'd done because I knew she would spank me for being careless.

She should have been fired.

In the fifth grade I and fifteen other ten year old boys were in love with our teacher. What a beautiful lady she was! And sweet to her students, too. But our dreams were shattered when she informed the class that she was to be married in three months. I'd never met her fiancé but I hated him for taking my secret sweetheart from me.

Another teacher in the sixth grade was not a very nice woman. She thrived on the prospect of spanking every child in her class with a paddle that seemed to be as big as a tennis racquet. I had the misfortune of being one of her victims.

Once when I was caught passing a note to my best friend she demanded that I bring it to her so that she could see what was written on the Blue

Horse notebook paper. I already knew what was there and I also knew I would be in trouble after she read it.

The request on the note was— NAME THREE PARTS OF A STOVE. The answer—LIFTER, LEG AND POKER. She didn't get it. It went right over her head. But the mere act of my passing the note warranted in her mind that I needed a paddling.

I got one in front of the entire class. That spanking didn't hurt at all but the embarrassment stung me so much that I stopped working in class.

CHAPTER FOUR

In the seventh grade my interest in basketball was beginning to grow with every shot I made. But no matter how much my game improved I still had to be concerned with my size. At four feet nothing tall I was in the dwarf category. I was short in stature, but my determination to make the team was as strong as any of the other boy's.

Before the 1940 season began the coach of our church team told me he had only ten uniforms and none small enough to fit me. After all, I was short enough to hear the grass grow so how could I possibly fit into a red, size twenty-eight jersey?

Not so easily discouraged, I asked Mother if she had any suggestions regarding my problem and, as usual, she had a possible solution. She remembered seeing sleeveless underwear shirts in various colors in a mail order catalog. Blue, green, and maroon were the only colors available.

When I asked her to show me what maroon looked like she pointed to a vase on an end table and said, "It's not red, but it's as close as we can get to it." She ordered the undershirt and two weeks later the long awaited jersey arrived. When I opened the package I saw a poor substitute for the Baptist's bright red uniforms. But it was at least a jersey and to make it look more like a basketball jersey we stuck a six inch strip of adhesive tape on the back to designate me as a number one. Number one? My name wasn't even on the coach's list as a player. Even though I was a bench warmer I still felt proud to sit with the coach and players during a game wearing my makeshift jersey.

Two years later I wore the official red church uniform and played as a starting guard with the big boys on our team. I began scoring points on the opposition and became the score leader on the squad that at one time didn't carry my name on the team roster.

Basketball was an important part of my junior high years but my mother had other plans for her eighth-grade child. She saw me as a concert pianist in the great concert halls, on world tours and wallowing in the glamour of stardom. With her expectations terribly high, she failed to remember that I hadn't had a lesson.

At fifty-cents a session, my teacher's instruction gave me the basic theory of music. I didn't like sitting for thirty minutes on a piano bench counting one and two and three and four on a practice song. But after a while I began taking her instruction with appreciation for the harmony that the eighty-eight notes produced on the piano.

A few of my friends laughed at me as I trudged to a piano lesson while they went to the baseball field for a pickup game. My ongoing fear was that my Mother would insist that I continue taking lessons until I began to shave.

But speaking of fear… recitals! Ouch! I despised the sound of the word. I'm sure I came to resent them because in my first one I completely forgot my piece smack-dab in the middle. And what a piece it was— "The Burning of Rome".

I'd guess that nobody in this hemisphere had ever heard that song. It was about Nero playing his fiddle while Rome burned. My disappointed teacher must have also burned when my fingers and mind stopped working at the same time.

My Mother's dream of having her son becoming a famous piano virtuoso died in the teacher's recital hall.

CHAPTER FIVE

In the mid-1940's Big Bottom seemed to have an unusually large number of boys compared to earlier years. And, as expected, many had their own quirks, mannerisms, habits, and normal attributes. For instance, Robert James began chewing acrid Red Ox chewing tobacco at age fourteen. The strong juice he spat could take varnish off interior door trim.

Then there was Ted Watson who smoked strong Avalon cigarettes before reaching ninth grade. He always smelled like campfire smoke.

Carl Toms had a harmless fetish for girl's angora sweaters and Tim Johnson cursed more than a drunk sailor in a stag bar.

Some of the other dozen or so boys tried to be noticed by doing awkward flips off the beech tree limb into the shallow river. Others hoped to draw attention by burning rubber off their parent's tires and swearing to mom and dad they hadn't gone over twenty miles an hour.

Despite minor shortcomings, the Big Bottom Boys held a measure of loyalty toward their hometown and the people who handled the day to day business. To them school was often boring. But if demeaned by outsiders to be second rate, each youngster would bow his neck and return a strong rebuttal. One of these prideful youngsters was Bart Wooten, youngest of four Wooten brothers who lived next door to us. Although he was from a good family with solid values, he felt he was living in the wrong century. He didn't fit in with the fast cars, stuck- up high school girls and boys his age who thought they were hot stuff.

Bart, age sixteen, would have been considerably more comfortable exploring the wilderness with Daniel Boone or Davy Crockett. Much to his displeasure he was hung in the middle of a World War II society with customs that simply didn't jive with his.

His first love was camping and hunting in the hills where he used his 30-30-gauge rifle to hone his shooting skills. He was never one to kill animals just for the thrill of killing. He would, however, take occasional shots at wild dogs carrying rabies, a disease that would eventually kill them.

Bart had twin toes, a five-foot-eight inch frame and toughness about him that younger boys envied. He often swam naked in the river, swimming to the opposite shore with one arm while carrying his clothes high out of the water with the other. All of us tried to follow his lead but somehow couldn't manage to keep our shirts and pants dry.

Bart was two years older than I and the same age as my brother Bobby. The two were fast friends who tried as best they could to keep me from tagging along to wherever they were going. It wasn't as if they didn't like me, they just felt that their maturity and interest levels were far above mine. In other words, I was a pest.

When I reached age fourteen both began accepting me as their equal in their goings on around the neighborhood. Their other Big Bottom friends were all of high school age. Some freshmen plus upperclassmen gave the group a wide range of maturity and a propensity to flirt with mischief.

My informal initiation into the group came on Halloween when I became a part of a prank that was extremely dangerous. But since I had recently become an accepted member of the Big Bottom clan I felt that I should go along with whatever was planned for the special evening.

What the Big Bottom Boys did to entertain themselves that holiday was undoubtedly unlawful. One of their tricks that went beyond innocence was blocking one end of Maple Street with a wrecked car.

A junk yard behind a car dealer's main building was filled with twenty or more automobiles that had run their final miles. With Bart, Bobby and me plus seven other neighborhood boys there was more than enough manpower to roll one of the junkers fifty feet to the street.

Once the car was deposited in the blocking position we hustled back to the lot to get another wreck rolling toward the street. Our plan was to put this car on its nose or grill and hold it there until an automobile stopped at the junker blocking the road. The second wreck was to be dropped behind the halted car leaving it stuck between two useless vehicles.

Keeping the second car on the nose-on-the-ground position wasn't easy. The slightest breeze made the old wreck sway from side to side. But the strength of nine young men was able to keep it balanced at least for a while.

Bart told me to run down to the end of the block and watch for any approaching vehicles. When I was certain that an oncoming car was heading for the roadblock I was to give a loud whistle signaling that the victim-to-be was headed straight toward the old car blocking the road.

"Whistle through your teeth so we can be sure to hear you," Bart told me. "After the car stops we won't have much time to drop this old wreck behind it."

"Yeah. Okay," I replied as I prepared to make my run. "I'll whistle as loud as I can. Don't worry about that."

"Good," Bart returned. "Now get yourself way down there near the Johnson's house and be ready to signal us. There should be a car coming' pretty soon," Bart encouraged. "A lot of traffic comes this way this time of the night."

Shortly after I had taken my position all talk and laughter stopped abruptly when every boy holding the car apparently heard my loud whistle coming from down the street. Bart reacted in a flash. "Okay, here comes what we've been waitin' for! Everybody hide behind the wreck as much as you can. We don't want to be spotted!"

Except for the squeaky sounds of the old wreck rocking back and forth and the grunting sounds of the boys straining to hold up the car, the area was creepy quiet.

"Here comes one for sure!" Bart said in a loud whisper. "Be ready to push your guts out when I give the signal to let'er go!"

The headlights of the approaching car gradually grew brighter as it neared the boys. It was coming at a slow pace and would soon be close enough for the driver to see the wreck blocking the road. Bart's concern was that the driver would see the old car then turn around and head back down Maple Street.

But the driver didn't turn around or shift to a slower speed. He kept coming until he was no more than two hundred feet from the boys. Heavy breathing attested that each was feeling not only the heavy load but also had a jumpy nervous system.

But they hung on and waited. Waited. Waited until the car passed in front of them and Bart gave his command.

"NOW!" he yelled. "TURN IT LOOSE!"

The second the car stopped at the blockade the boys gave the strongest push they could give. The upright junker slammed onto the concrete no more than ten feet behind the idling victim. They had finished the job as planned. Now they had to start running at top speed to get away from the bizarre scene they had created.

However.

As they rushed to leave the car lot Bobby glanced back at the hemmed in vehicle under the street light and saw something that shot an arrow of fear into his heart.

A large star.

On the outside of the passenger side door.

Beneath it, the word "SHERIFF".

Bobby immediately began yelling at me and our buddies as we approached the sandy path by the river.

"IT'S THE SHERIFF!" he shouted at the ones running ahead of him. "WE'VE BLOCKED IN THE DAMN SHERIFF!!!"

Before Bobby or any of his buddies could say anything else to each other, a chilling sound rang out coming from the direction of the stalled car.

"POW! POW! POW!"

Pistol shots.

Sounding to be aimed in our direction.

The rapid gait we had set suddenly increased from simple trotting into what would certainly be acceptable times in a one hundred yard dash. Our feet were moving so quickly that storms of loose sand flew behind each of us into the trailing boys' faces and bodies.

"FASTER!" Bobby yelled to runners in front of him. "WE HAVE TO GET AS FAR AWAY AS WE CAN RIGHT NOW!!"

One or more questions had to be zipping through our disturbed brains: If the sheriff gets out of our trap will he be coming after us? Or is he stuck between the two wrecks and will need help to get out?

Bart, running near the front of the pack, turned to us and said in gasps,

"WE CAN'T STAY...ON THIS PATH MUCH LONGER. GET OFF THE RIVERBANK!...HEAD FOR HOME...AND STAY THERE!!! THE LAW KNOWS EXACTLY... WHERE WE ARE."

"DID EVERYBODY HEAR BART?" Bobby called out to the rest of us. "DO WHAT HE SAYS AND GET YOUR BUTTS HOME! THE SHERIFF HAS NO IDEA WHO SET THE TRAP AGAINST HIM SO FEEL SAFE!"

The wacky night ended with all the boys vowing they would never set another blockade with two junkers. Bart ended his part of the conversation for the evening saying, "Two junkers? Nah. I'm thinkin' that we'll probably go back to using one and only one."

"You're nutty," Rabbit Morse accused. "There ain't gonna' be anymore street blockin' for me. From now on I'm changin' my ways and goin' trick or treatin' with the little ones. I might even ask the sheriff to go with us."

So ended the first major involvement with my seniors without being called a tag along. As scary as the street blocking was I look back on it now as a chance for me to get into their neighborhood fraternity.

CHAPTER SIX

When the Japanese bombed Pearl Harbor I can remember to this day where I was when the announcement was made. I would guess that everyone living then could do the same thing.

I was shooting baskets on an outdoor basketball court with friends when the Revered H.G.M Hatler yelled at us from his front porch. From a fair distance away he told us that Pearl Harbor had been attacked by the Japanese.

At the time I really didn't know if what the Reverend told us was good or bad. I'd never heard of Pearl Harbor and all I knew about the Japanese was that they made tin toys and ate with little sticks.

In order to find more about the bombing we went to Ross Bailey's house to talk to his parents. When we went in the front door we saw Ross' dad sitting in his easy chair listening to one of the network's newscasters. He looked angry.

"Those sneaky little bastards have gone and done it now," Mr. Bailey volunteered as each of us took a seat on the floor. "They've been mad as all get out at us ever since we cut off their oil supply. Now they want to take over this country so they can get all they want. Damn them away, the slit-eyed little varmints."

I think all of us knew that the bombing of Pearl Harbor was going to throw us into a conflict with Japan. They were fully prepared to go to war. But America, later to be called "a sleeping giant", had been caught with its pants down.

At home that night I asked my parents more questions about the terrible events of the day but found that they knew about as much as I did about what was going on. Our radio stayed on most of the night. Nearly all the stations were commenting on the Japanese attack and guessing what was to come next for this country.

CHAPTER SEVEN

In the 1944 high school marching band there were only twenty players left after the draft took a good many of them. The band director had to recruit younger players to help fill out the skeleton crew that was left to march and play (however poorly). This was when I became a drummer in the band at age fourteen.

Due to lack of experience in both marching and playing the band had little to brag about. They were at their best when marching but not playing.

There were rare times, however, when the band sounded pretty good. That occurred once when we stood on the doorsteps of the old courthouse and played for the men going off to war.

I remember seeing people crying as they watched their sons leave home, some for the first time in their lives. Some or all of them would probably be called to fight in unheard of places such as Iwo Jima, Saipan, the bulge, Okinawa, and other god-awful battlefields.

As we played "The Star Spangled Banner" I watched the emotions of the onlookers and tried as much as possible to read the sad faces of those being left behind. Even at my age I could feel some of the misery they felt as their sons disappeared into the waiting bus.

As a token of the town's appreciation for the departing boys, Don Fouts owner of the drug store where the boys used to hang out, handed each recruit a carton of Lucky Strike cigarettes and a smile.

I don't think I was mature enough to feel the full blast of emotions that the relatives and friends were experiencing. But I knew this scene was different from any I had ever been around. I think that as a fourteen year old, I grew up a notch in that thirty-minute scene in front of the courthouse.

CHAPTER EIGHT

Helen, Lois, Tina, Mary, Betty, Ella, Rita, Nancy, Tom, R.L., Sammy, and Donnie Banks: at one time or another these sisters and brothers lived in the same house in Big Bottom. In the front window of their home hung a small red, white and blue banner holding four blue stars. Each star represented a family member who was serving or had served in the armed forces. R.L., next to the youngest, was discharged due to injuries incurred in a jeep wreck while on duty in the Army.

When each of the twelve children was born he and she were welcomed into the world with the word "work". Without a doubt these loyal Americans were the hardest working people in Perry County or any other county close by. In their daily labors they tore down buildings, hauled anything in their trucks from bricks to horse manure, and pushed dirt and rocks all over the county with heavy machinery.

R.L. was a patriotic young man. Much of his love for his county came from his dad, Samuel Banks. The elder Banks once attacked and personally whipped two leftfield religious men for not honoring the American flag as it passed by them in a parade. When they didn't remove their hats, Samuel removed them for them.

When the call came for citizens to help collect scrap for the war effort, R.L. was ready. In his large panel truck he planned to find and deliver rubber tires, tinfoil, lead pipe, and other appropriate materials to a collection area in front of the courthouse.

He decided to recruit some of the Big Bottom boys he knew who were good workers and would want to help the worthy project. He contacted five boys he felt would be interested in working with him for the next three days. Sammy Hurst, Bobby McGuire, Billy "Rabbit" Morse, Bart Wooten and I didn't hesitate to say yes when we were asked.

The day before the scrap drive began R.L. met with us and doled out orders like a frontline combat sergeant.

"Now listen to me," he began, "Everybody in town is going to try to collect more junk than their neighbors or anybody else working against them. But I'll tell you what, we're gonna' change the key of that little tune and show folks who really knows how to fill up a truck. I want all of you to meet me at Lou Canter's garage at eight o'clock in the morning. He's already pointed out to me what we can and can't take as scrap. It'll be a good start for us. Then we'll go to Fleenor's garage and tear into his wrecked cars for metal stuff that can't be used anymore. Any questions?"

"Yeah, I have two," Bobby responded. "How long will the collectin' last and do you really think we can beat everybody in town?"

"Good questions, Bobby," R.L. returned. "It's a three day thing and I know where we can get more damn junk than anybody could ever dream about. Yeah, three days. That's what it's gonna' be. That'll be enough time to bear down and whip everybody's rear end that's goin' up against us. Look, our six will beat any collector and you can bet your last quarter that the town's gonna' be chasin' us. I wouldn't have it any other way. Let'em chase."

At eight o'clock the following morning, R.L. stood on the back edge of the truck bed and gave final orders to his troops. He talked and we listened.

"Now, the first thing we gotta' do is to be careful and take only the junk pieces that I tell you to. You got that?"

All five nodded yes.

"You have to be careful," R.L. warned. "Some of the pieces you'll handle are goin' to have sharp, jagged edges and can cut the tar out of you. So keep that in mind when you start your liftin' and carryin'. If nobody's got any questions then let's get to it." R.L. ordered.

"Bobby, you and Tim head to the lot directly behind the garage. There's a bunch of stuff there and some of it's real heavy. Try not to strain out a hernia," he said, smiling.

"Sammy, you and Rabbit go across Maple Street to the area where Lou has pitched a ton or more of his junk metal. There's a bunch of scrap there so take your time and start bringin' it to me."

"We're gone," Sammy said. "We'll be back with our first load in no more than ten minutes."

"All right, Sammy. Get to it."

Now I was the only one left to receive instructions and because of my size I was afraid I wouldn't be included on the collection team. I guess R.L. thought that my small frame and slender arms were limited in what they could lift and carry.

After waiting a few seconds to pose my question, I finally looked up at R.L. standing on the truck and began speaking my piece.

"Okay, R.L. where you goin' to send me? I can lift too, you know."

"I know that, Don," R.L. replied. "And there's an important place for you in this operation. Tell you what, go and start lookin' for the pieces that are really valuable in this scrap drive."

"What kind of pieces?"

"Chrome," R.L. responded. "It's as valuable as all get out and you can find tons of it scattered in small pieces all over the lots. It won't be too heavy for you to handle."

"Chrome?" I asked curiously.

"Yeah, chrome, Don. You know, it's that real shiny silver looking metal that's on grills, bumpers, and door handles. That's a perfect job for you so get goin' and bring somethin' to load onto this truck."

Of course R.L. had no hint of a clue that chrome was more valuable than ordinary metal. He just wanted to involve me in the metal scavenger hunt.

"Thanks R.L.," I said as I turned and started in a fast trot toward the junk lot. I was excited about doing my part to make a clean sweep of all the chrome pieces I could find.

By five o'clock the R.L. crew had made three trips to the unloading area at the courthouse. Every imaginable description of metal was included in each delivery: car doors, fenders, tires, metal barrels—these and other collectible pieces came from four car dealerships and several mechanics' repair shops.

However, with all the carrying and hauling of the long day something landed a crippling blow to each of us—fatigue. When the final piece of junk was unloaded we flopped like rag dolls onto the truck bed. All five of us were prostrate, pooped, and looking forward to stepping into a tub of cool water at home.

R.L. drove us back to our starting point at Lou Canter's garage and before leaving for home gave us a brief critique of our collection day.

"You all look like a bunch of scallywags," he began to us sitting on the street curb. "You're filthy, worn out, and I'm sure ready to eat the meal you missed at noon today. But let me tell you this, no matter how you look and feel I have to admit that I've never worked with anybody who gave as much muscle and dedication as you five did today. I know your folks are goin' be proud when they hear what this crew did in eight hours."

All of us were silent. Our heads drooped from weariness. Each smelled like the bottom of a garbage can and, predictably, no one knew how to respond to R.L.'s compliment. Bobby finally made an attempt to reply to our leader.

"Uh, R.L., we aren't trying to be heroes. Ya' know collectin' all that junk was harder than we thought it would be. But now that we've finished I think all of us feel pretty good about what we've done. The next two days should be a little easier now that we know a lot better how to handle the heavy stuff."

At that point Tom entered the discussion.

"R.L., we know you had the hardest job of all today. You had to handle every single piece of junk that we carried to the truck. Every piece. And you had to stack it in the right places to make sure there was no wasted space. We carried only one piece at a time but you had to handle all of it."

"Okay, that's enough Tom," R.L. replied trying to get out of the spotlight. "We all worked hard and Lord willin' we'll do it again tomorrow."

CHAPTER NINE

The second day of the scrap drive was somewhat the same as the day before. But on the third and final day we swore to work harder and get as much metal as we could before the drive ended.

For a change R.L. decided to leave the city limits and search for junk in the small surrounding communities. We rode for an hour or so looking for anything that would qualify as acceptable material back at the courthouse. Then out of the blue we hit paydirt.

At Duane (also called Pistol City) we found a virtual gold mine of old metal that had been discarded by someone connected to worked-out mines. At the community's only filling station we asked who owned the old mine and the proprietor said, "The owner wasn't local and when he ran out of coal he left town swearin' never to come back. We've been tryin' to get rid of that eyesore of stacked metal but can't find anybody who wants it."

"You've found somebody now," R.L. returned. "We'll take it off your hands and give it all to the government for making war materials. It'll be gone by dark."

In less than four hours we loaded and hauled three truckloads of newfound metal to the courthouse. We had discovered the mother lode of available junk and if anyone came close to matching our tonnage we would be shocked.

At six o'clock, three days after the scrap collection began it was over. Evidence of the town's effort to find materials for the Armed Services could be seen in the huge amount of stacked scrap stretching more than one city block. The entire county had kicked in to make the area proud of itself.

It had gone beyond the call of patriotism to exceed the tonnage numbers assigned to them. One would like to think that Oliver Hazard Perry would have been mighty proud of his people.

After we finished unloading our final truck full of scrap we headed for home. Weariness that had swallowed us the first day of collection was again in our bones. The success we had experienced with R.L.'s well planned campaign had boosted our morale, enthusiasm, and pride. We realized we had done something very important and being proud was justified by our effort.

When the final tonnage figures were totaled our bunch had brought 10,000 pounds of scrap to the courthouse. That averaged out to 2,000 pounds for each Big Bottom boy. Not bad when considering that each citizen was expected to collect and deliver only one hundred pounds.

R.L.'s team suddenly became a serious item for the locals to talk about. So serious that the Hazard Herald, a weekly publication, wrote a brief article regarding the Big Bottom Boys' remarkable effort in the junk collection campaign.

How and why did we do it? The answer comes easy now. Each of us knew what war is. We were aware that many of our neighbors were dodging bullets and digging foxholes to hide from the enemy's gunfire. We were old enough to realize that battle equipment had to come from somewhere. And a part of the somewhere was in small town U.S.A— Hazard, Kentucky.

When Bobby and I got home from the courthouse we trudged into the living room dirty, stinking, and completely out of gas. Three days— a heck of a long time to lift and carry junk to R.L.'s truck. With all the energy expended I doubted if I had enough strength left to undress and flop into the bathtub and stay for a week or more.

Mother came out of the kitchen when she heard Bobby and me come in the front door. As she took her first look at us I could tell she as within a hair of breaking a tear. There we stood. Her boys who hadn't the slightest idea where Germany or Japan were had given every ounce of their energy to help men and women fight a war.

She gave us a light kiss on our foreheads, a love pat on both our rear ends and said, "Now get to the bathroom, take off those stinking clothes and try to wash all the grime and grease off your bodies."

23

Thirty minutes later after finishing scrubbing ourselves we sat at the supper table where we began feeling the vigor of youth retuning to our bodies. A day of accomplishment was coming to an end. Without realizing it the Big Bottom Boys had become heroes in our community. We hadn't planned it that way but it happened and we were pleased that it did.

CHAPTER TEN

Best friends come in small numbers. If you have one you're fortunate. Two, you are indeed blessed. And having, say, five you are a highly favored person. Glen "Wennie" Maggard was a best friend. We were born two weeks apart, went to first grade together and kept a close relationship through our adult years. Our wives and children were also close. When we were together the talk was mostly about the young ones: how they were doing in school, who did what, when or where.

But in our early teen years there were times when I didn't like Glen. He went out of his way more than once to scare the devil out of me at his dad's funeral home. The tricks he threw at me temporarily broke any bond that had existed between us since childhood.

Around age fifteen I made a vow that I would never go inside the Maggard and Johnson Funeral Home. If forced to go I knew there would be some sort of joke or scare waiting for me.

One year earlier Glen and his father Earl locked James Jenkins and me inside the casket room and started making eerie howling sounds through the cracks in the main door. I think James and I lost our water.

In pitch darkness we felt our way around for a minute or two until we reached the double doors leading to the outside. Once there, James began screaming, "LET US OUTTA HERE, WEENIE! IT AIN'T FUNNY! OPEN THIS DAMN DOOR!"

But Weenie didn't have to unlock the door. It was already unlocked. All we had to do was push very gently to let in the afternoon sunshine.

"The little fizzle," I called Glen out loud as James and I quickly stepped out the door and trotted away from the funeral home. "I'm goin' to get even with him for doin' this to us. Just wait. I'll get him."

We had no idea that Glen and his dad were laughing as they watched us hurry away. James and I weren't laughing. We were happy to get as far away as possible from someone who was supposed to be one of our best friends. At the moment I didn't give a hoot about him.

CHAPTER ELEVEN

Weeks after the casket room lock- in I had regained enough courage to visit Gene and his dad on the front porch of the funeral home. Not inside. After a few minutes I became interested in what Glen was saying about his liquor drinking cousin, Tom Deaton.

Seems that Tom got completely auger-eyed drunk every Saturday of the week and invariably ended up trying to sleep it off on one of the funeral home's backroom couches.

Like good relatives would do, Glen and his dad let Tom take whatever time he needed to come out of his self induced coma. He was never in the way of any visitation or funerals and Earl wanted to keep it that way.

One spring Saturday in 1950 Tom made his usual trek to the funeral home to sleep off his weekly alcohol consumption. I happened to be there helping Glen wash one of the ambulances when he staggered through the front door and weaved his way to his familiar couch.

Earl watched his nephew fall like a rock onto the cushions noticing that Tom seemed to be more inebriated than on previous Saturdays. He called Glen and me into the main office to tell us he had a plan to halt Tom's weekly routine. Knowing the tricks that Earl could and would play I was curious to hear what he was planning for his passed out relative.

"Tell you what we're goin' to do," Earl began. "I want both of you to go to the casket room and wheel out that grey unit into the main parlor. Be quiet about it. And when you're through come back and go with me to Tom's couch. We're gonna' carry that drunk sonofagun and drop him in the casket you'll bring in."

"Do what?" I asked. "We're gonna' do what?"

"We're gonna' put ol' Tom in repose, put the purple and yellow lights on him and turn on "Amazing Grace". That's what we're gonna' do."

"Oh no we're not," I answered quickly. "I don't want to be a part of what you're plannin'. I might watch but that's all."

"Have it your way, chicken, but stay out of our way," Glen replied as he looked toward his father. "You know, Dad, Tom's pretty heavy. You don't think he'll wake up while we're liftin' and draggin' him on the floor?"

"A twenty gun salute wouldn't wake up ol' Tom with the shape he's in," Earl assured. "Now go get the casket and roll it to the chapel. Let's get the drunkard in his coffin so we can pay our final respects."

It took about five minutes to move Tom from the couch to the waiting casket. He didn't move a muscle or come close to waking up. In fact, he snored while they carried him.

Finally at the coffin they struggled lifting him off the floor and rolling him over the edge onto the cushions. Earl then crossed Tom's hands near his belt and closed the bottom half of the casket.

"Now, let's go sit on the couch and watch our shocked relative come back to life," Earl suggested. "It may take an hour or more for the hooch to wear off but we can wait."

I wasn't sure how to take all these weird goings on. Tom was a good friend and I felt some guilt in what would undoubtedly be demeaning to him when he realized what had happened. But that was the way Glen and his dad loved to play jokes on their relatives and friends.

The hour passed slowly. Cars going past the front of the funeral home were the only sound coming inside the mortuary. To break the silence Earl turned on recorded hymns normally played at a real wake.

The scene was set for the great awakening. Forty-five minutes had passed since Tom became a living corpse. The three of us on the couch kept looking at his hands and head, watching for any hint of movement that might signal that he was coming back to reality.

Then it finally happened. His hands moved first. Next, his head turned slowly to the left side and repeated its turn to the right. Tom was in the first stage of waking up and Earl and Glen on the couch were beginning to giggle at his first move. I didn't giggle.

The next movement from the coffin brought Tom back to be among the living. He opened his eyes, looked up at the ceiling and squinted as if to ask himself, "Where in the hell am I?" He finally spoke loud enough for the three of us to hear his concern about where he was and how he got there.

"Where in the hell am I?" he finally spoke without lifting his head off the silk pillow. "I ain't on my couch. What did you do to me?"

"Didn't do anything, Tom. You died yesterday," Earl joked.

"Died? Hell, I'm just as alive as you sonsabitches and I'll show you that I am."

With that response Tom began tearing the casket bedding away from his sides then reached and opened the bottom half of the lid. His next move was similar to a rider dismounting a horse—left leg over the side of the casket until it hit the floor. Right one follows.. Tom was out of his metal confines apparently ready to vent his anger toward the three of us sitting on the couch.

Still heavily under the influence of his Saturday imbibing, he started a swerving walk away from his casket toward the three of us. He was mumbling something or other. We couldn't make out what it was but we knew for sure it wasn't words of compassion for his relatives and friend.

"I'll say it one more time, you're a bunch of sonsabitches for doing what you just did to me. I ain't never comin' back to this friggin' place. Never." He ended with a loud hiccup.

We couldn't tell if he was going to tear into us or keep staggering toward the door. Seeing that he was still having trouble keeping his balance, I got up and went to help him.

As far as I know Tom never tried to get even with Earl and Glen. I think he knew that I had refused to be a part of the casket scene. And for that he always showed a special respect for me. I encouraged him to go home and finish sobering up. He broke a little smile at me and said, "I really ain't mad at nobody (hiccup). Just a little surprised that the three of you made a jackass out of me for a few minutes. But, that's okay (hiccup #2). I'm just gonna' go somewhere else and find me another couch."

CHAPTER TWELVE

In early October, 1944, a special notice was issued by Family theatre owners announcing that Hollywood's famous Western cowboy, Tex Ritter, was coming to Hazard with his show. Somehow, someway, Mr. Ritter would be traveling nearly three thousand miles to perform in a town with a population of not more than five thousand residents.

Colorful posters announcing Tex's performance had been posted on virtually every telephone pole and flat surface in town that the theatre employees could reach. On three by three placards in bold red, white and blue letters they read:

IN PERSON
TEX RITTER IS COMING TO THE
FAMILY THEATRE WITH HIS ALL
WESTERN SHOW OCTOBER 24, 1944.
2:00 P.M. TICKETS $1.00 FOR 18
AND UNDER $1.50 ADULTS
COME SEE HOLLYWOOD'S MOST
POPULAR COWBOY AND THE RENOWNED
SONS OF THE PIONNERS SINGING
THEIR POPULAR SONGS.

And so the date was set for a famous cowboy movie star to come to Hazard in less than three weeks. No star bigger than Tex Ritter and his big Western show had ever crossed the border into Perry County. Most of the citizens of the town and county were still having trouble believing they would have a chance to see and hear a bonafied hero of the silver screen.

The problem for the Big Bottom Boys as well as the other youngsters in town was coming up with the price of admission. One dollar was an out of sight premium to pay to see Tex Ritter, Enrico Caruso, Frank Sinatra or any other celebrity in a staged event. The boys would certainly have to go on bended knee, to grovel and swear to heaven not to ever smoke cigarettes again. They would gladly do these things if their parents would cough up the price of admission. With the event more than twenty days away the youngsters still had plenty of time to search for ways to get into their mom and dad's pocketbooks.

CHAPTER THIRTEEN

The big day finally arrived and the town was all abuzz about Tex Ritter's show. A few fans had already staked their claim by standing in line at the ticket window at 9:30 A.M. They were determined that no one was going to beat them getting the best seats in the house. The early enthusiasm probably indicated that the place would be full when Tex began dispensing his celebrity talents to the locals at 2:00 P.M.

Bobby and I successfully talked our parents into footing the bill for the show. It took a lot of begging to get them to fork up the price of admission but they finally came through with what we needed.

Most of the boys and girls interested in the show were also successful in convincing their folks that the show was a once in a lifetime chance for them to see such a famous movie star. But Bart was having trouble finding the price of admission at home or at his dad's worksite on Cedar Street.

At noon, he, Bobby and I were looking down into a large hole Mr. Wooten, a hardnosed plumber, had dug searching for a broken water line. The hole was deeper than most of the ones he had dug in the past on similar jobs. He was in an awkward, bent over position struggling to dig and pitch dirt out of the deepening hole.

We could hear him groaning and grunting with every shovelful he heaved onto the ground above him. Obviously it wasn't the best time to confront Mr. Wooten with trivial matters. But it had to be done and Bart began his effort to get a dollar bill from his dad's pocket into his. He knew it wouldn't be easy to do.

"Dad," Bart began. "I need to talk to you."

No response came from the sweating man in the hole.

"Hey Dad," Bart called louder. "Look up here. I want to ask you something."

"I hear you, Bart," his dad returned. "Can't you see that I'm busy. Now go on and get away from here. I don't have time to deal with your foolishness."

"What I'm going to ask you is not foolish. I just want you to give me a dollar so I can go with Bobby and Don to see Tex Ritter."

"Tex who?"

"Ritter. Tex Ritter, the cowboy."

"I don't have a dollar to waste on any cowboy."

"It's not wastin'. He's a movie star and I really want to see him."

"Well then, if that's what you're interested in then go find a picture of him and look all you want."

"Come on, Dad," Bart urged in increasing decibels. "This is the only time I've ever asked you for that much money to see a show. Break down and pitch a dollar up here."

"Bart!" Mr. Wooten hollered loudly, still bending down inside the hole. "Get the hell away from here. I'm not giving you a dollar or even half a dollar. Now scat!"

"For the last time, let me have the money. Please Dad."

"No!" the return came loudly from the hole. "I'm through talkin'. Get gone."

"Okay," Bart replied. "I'm goin' but I want to leave you somethin' to remember me by. And here it is."

With his final words Bart began kicking dirt into the hole and on top of his dad's back. He kept kicking until Mr. Wooten straightened up, spat out dirt and threw a few chosen words to his son.

"Why you little fart. I'm goin' to bust your hide," Mr. Wooten said as he began climbing out of the hole. "You won't get away with this trick."

"Goodbye, daddy Bill," Bart said as the three of us turned and broke into a fast run away from the work site. We would not be caught by a sixty-year-old plumber. However, sooner or later Bart would have to go home and face whatever punishment his dad would be waiting to dish out. But for now he had to search quickly for a prospective dollar donor.

Time was running out with Mr. Ritter's show now only two hours away from opening.

Bart wanted to kiss his sister Billie when she handed him the coveted one dollar bill he thought would never hit the inside of his pocket. Grudgingly she had reached into her purse while demanding that her little brother made a cross-my-heart promise to pay back the loan as soon as possible.

"I promise, Billie. I swear I do," Bart returned humbly. "As soon as I can cut Fred Crutchfield's grass you'll get your money back."

"You'd better live up to that promise Mr. Bart or I'll break your neck and maybe some other body parts, too."

"I sure do thank you sister," Bart replied gratefully as he took the money. "You're the only one I could count on to help me out and I won't be forgettin' it."

CHAPTER FOURTEEN

At one o'clock all the Big Bottom Boys were in a long line leading to the theatre box office. Ahead were twenty or so people anxiously waiting for the ticket lady to begin selling tickets. To the boys she had always been the extra special one who could give them passage to see untouchable movie stars on thirty-five millimeter film.

She was also the distributor of passports in ticket form that took them around the world to strange and wonderful places they had never heard of. And most comforting to know she was there every day of the week always available to offer new viewing experiences to anyone with the price of admission. The ticket lady was the only person in town who could allow the citizens to take a break from their daily routines for a few minutes and find a magic world inside a movie theatre.

The Family Theatre did have a problem getting up- to- date films. Some of the movies they received from the film distributing companies were six months or more old. When the movies didn't arrive on time the theatre management would offer the audiences the same movie they showed the last time the films were late getting to Hazard.

Held in reserve was the picture "The Jungle Princess" which was shown at least a dozen times a year. Some of the customers came back time after time to see the voluptuous female star with the body and face of a Greek goddess.

But today there was no old film to pull customers into the theatre. Instead there was a live, singing movie star with a Western show for ticket holders to enjoy.

At 1:30 sharp the venetian blind on the ticket window suddenly opened. The magic lady behind the glass window began selling show tickets fast and furiously. In less than five minutes, all the Big Bottom Boys had their tickets in hand and were inside the room that would undoubtedly be jammed with people within the next few minutes.

We took our seats in an aisle close to the middle of the theatre and immediately noticed that something was different about the interior of the room.

Somebody had swept the floor, maybe even mopped it. Also, the ever present stink that could curl a head of straight hair was gone. Someone must have used gallons of deodorant to clean the air. Now the interior smelled like an over ripe Georgia peach. We were shocked at the changes.

Five minutes till showtime.

Conversations gradually became quieter. Loud talk diminished to excited whispers as the audience seemed to sense that things were about to get underway. And they were.

The few houselights that had been burning since the doors opened for business suddenly went dark. The second the lights dimmed the full house of enthusiastic Tex Ritter fans burst out with loud cheers and enthusiastic applause that could probably be heard blocks away.

They knew the opening was near when silhouettes of the musicians began moving about the darkened stage. Then the deep voice of the show's announcer came over the loudspeaker setting the scene for the arrival of the star performer…

LADIES AND GENTLEMEN WELCOME TO THE FAMILY THEATRE AND TO AN AFTERNOON OF GREAT ENTERTAINMENT BY MOVIELAND'S MOST POPULAR COWBOY. HE HAS APPEARED ALL OVER AMERICA AS WELL AS IN FOREIGN COUNTRIES AROUND THE WORLD. HE IS HOLLYWOOD'S MOST BELOVED WESTERN STAR. WITHOUT FURTHER ADO, PLEASE WELCOME TO YOUR TOWN AND THIS THEATRE THE ONE AND ONLY…TEX RITTER!!!

The moment the announcer said Tex Ritter all the house lights went up to peak brightness. The cheering and screaming were deafening, drowning out the introductory music coming from the stage. And then the long awaited moment arrived as the man himself came walking down the aisle on the right side of the theatre. He was smiling as if he had discovered a slice of paradise and waved to the crowd with his cowboy hat in hand stretching above his head.

Slowly, Tex made his way toward the stage passing the aisle seat where I was sitting. The star was close enough for me to touch with an extended hand. I was squeezing my rump cheeks together to keep from peeing in my pants. I couldn't smile. I couldn't speak. All I and the other boys could do was stare in disbelief at the man with a silver, pearl handle pistol sticking out of a beautifully crafted holster. His cowboy hat looked to be as big as a number three washtub.

The star approached the stage where his musicians were blasting out the show's introductory song. The crowd was wild. Their volume was probably off the high end of the decibel scale. With knee jerk reaction they came to their feet applauding the man everyone in the house was acquainted with through all his Saturday afternoon movies they had seen over the years.

The applause escalated even more as Tex reached the stage and walked toward the microphone. Once there he continued to wave his white hat to the audience. And he kept smiling as if his day was now complete for having met his Hazard fans.

The noisy applause softened as the star strapped on his guitar and began singing one of his biggest hits. Everyone in the theatre knew the song and most pantomimed the words along with Tex's rendition.

"RYE WHISKEY, RYE WHISKEY, RYE WHISKEY I CRY, IF I don't GET RYE WHISKEY I THINK I WILL DIE."

The response to the cowboy's opening song was loud as it had been when Tex entered the theatre. Still standing, the crowd clapped along with the rhythm of the tune. They had cheered themselves into a mild frenzy prompted by the charismatic man who seemed to be singing a personal message to each individual in the house.

When the opening song ended, the enthusiastic fans took their seats anxiously to see what was to come next. After weeks of waiting for the star to come to Hazard the loyal fans were actually seeing Tex Ritter standing there looking down at his fans through the bright spotlight that lit up the man from movieland. Unbelievable. It seemed that no one in the audience could realize they were seeing in person the good guy who always won out over the bad characters in his movies. But there he was, bigger than life, ready to spin his magic.

Tex sang two more of his well-known songs then introduced the crowd to the popular singing group, The Sons of the Pioneers. They had performed with other Western stars such as Roy Rogers and Gene Autry and had signed on with Mr. Ritter to do a series of road shows.

The first song they sang was undoubtedly their biggest hit—"Drifting Along With The Tumbling Tumble Weed". Everybody in the audience seemed to know the song from hearing it sung so often on the screen and over the radio. It was the group's signature song. The next tune, "Cool, Cool Water" drew as much applause as the opening tune.

Following songs by the show's lady singers, Tex once again took charge of the production. He sang a medley of his best-known hits and was greeted at the finish by another round of enthusiastic applause.

All of us were still in a state of shock from seeing the star and all the trappings of the show. Their most thrilling moment came when at the conclusion of his last song Tex walked toward the left wing of the theatre and disappeared for a few seconds. When he reappeared he was leading his famous horse White Flash onto the stage. This was the same animal that galloped in front of us in all Tex Ritter movies we had seen.

The beautiful horse was as white as late December snow. The saddle he carried was deep black garnished with an array of attractive silver appointments from front to back and top to bottom. The bridle was also black with glistening rhinestones that contrasted with the white head and dark eyes of the imposing animal.

One problem White Flash showed was a natural response that most horses release in anxiety when appearing before large, noisy crowds. With his ears drawn back and look of pure pleasure in his eyes he released a huge pile of horse dung smack dab in the center of the stage. None of the cast including Tex paid attention to the horse's expulsion. They had seen the same thing happen in shows so many times that the scene had become second nature to them.

In no more than ten seconds one of the hired hands trotted on stage, scooped up the pile in one swoop with a large shovel then disappeared into the wings. Of course the horse's bowel relief created a small wave of laughter throughout the audience. But no one seemed to mind that the animal's natural calling had been satisfied in front of their eyes.

The show continued with rope tricks, fast pistol draws between Tex and one of his men and a comedy routine by a funny comedian. Bart, Bobby, and Rabbit, not being western music fans, enjoyed the roping, pistol drawings and jokes more than the lineup of songs. To them cowboys weren't supposed to be singers. Their purpose of being on film was to overcome whatever manner of evil they had to face with fists and guns. Singing was for sissies.

As the show approached its finale Tex created the most exiting scene of the day. The Sons of Pioneers played and sang their final song as he climbed onto White Flash. With a gentle pull of the reins the well-trained animal reared up on his back legs and pawed the air with his front hooves. Tex removed his hat and waved it to the crowd a final time to show his appreciation for their positive response to his show.

Then to end it all literally with a bang, the star pulled his pistol from the holster and fired six deafening blank bullets into the air above his head. The girls screamed and covered their ears far too late. The boys yelled a bunch of "Yeahs!" and "Do it again Tex!" as the smoke from the pistol partially hid the stage from the audience.

Tex was still waving and smiling as he backed his horse a few feet and disappeared behind the closing curtain. The crowd wanted to see their hero a final time before leaving the theatre. So instead of vacating their seats they kept clapping for a curtain call.

The cowboy star honored their wish as the curtain opened for a final time and White Flash bowed to his knees as if to say "Thank you". Then, the once in an eternity show was over. A few diehard customers kept clapping for another encore. But five minutes after the finale Tex was already out of the building. The crowd began leaving their seats and walking toward the exits reviewing all they had seen and heard in the exciting show.

"How in the hell did he train that horse to bow?" Bart asked us as we filed out of the theatre. "It must have taken a heck of a long time to get that big animal to do such a trick."

"Probably did," Bobby responded. "They must have used a sledge hammer on his knees to get him to bend or at least a two by four. Whatever they used really did the job."

Before going home, we made our customary stop at Don's Drug for a five cent Coke chilled by the owner's special crushed ice. It was standard procedure for most of the teenagers to stop for a while at the drugstore following a movie and talk about the plus and minus features of what they had just seen.

But that night's caucus wouldn't concern a movie but instead a review of the appearance of a Hollywood star. How important it was to have the opportunity to critique the appearance of a big time professional actor on a white horse.

Final note: Bart felt the sting of a razor strop on his rump as soon as he walked in the front door of his house. Plumber Wooten was punishing his son for kicking dirt onto his back because he wouldn't give Bart one dollar to see Tex.

CHAPTER FIFTEEN

Entering high school was a big day for me. Maybe it still is for most youngsters. I think the things that impressed me most was how physically developed both the boys and girls were. I mean the girls looked as old as my aunts and one or two even had babies! WOW! Now that was heavy stuff for a naïve freshman to handle.

Most of the boys wore tight fitting dungarees, told dirty jokes and cursed quite a bit. I really didn't have any desire to be like them. As for me, I was a five-feet-six-inches powderpuff next to those big people. But I was a proud littlin' as some of the upperclassmen called me.

Superintendent Whittinghill and Principal Eversole impressed me more than the President of the United States and Buck Jones, the movie cowboy. I was scared stiff of both of them. And the teachers— they seemed to have a level of sophistication I never saw in my elementary teachers.

Just as I was settling into my day to day routine in our school, possibly the worst news I'd ever heard in my life hit me like a Joe Louis right cross.

James Lester Ward, age sixteen, good tenth grade student, friendly, a buddy of mine was killed in a car wreck that could have been prevented had a stupid teenage driver not been showing off. The car couldn't make a steep curve, turned over and rolled on top of my friend who had been thrown from the car.

How did the sixteen-year-old friends of James handle such an emotional shock? I didn't know at the time. I can remember the confusion I felt when I looked at James in his casket and thought— where is he now?

I sometimes think about James and wonder what he would be doing today if he were alive. I also think of how much he's missed by not being around.

Today I question if high school kids are equipped to deal with some of the emotional situations they face. Most problems they handle. Some they don't. And the one that stymies the mind either mature or otherwise is death.

CHAPTER SIXTEEN

The Hazard High School football team practiced and played on the worst field imaginable. There was no grass, plenty of loose rocks, and a drop off of twenty-feet or more behind the goalpost at one end of the field.

In the ninth grade I was head equipment manager for the football team. My job was to make certain that each player had the proper equipment to compete with his own players as well as the team he would be playing against in the fall.

Paintsville, Prestonsburg, Pikeville, Hazard and Corbin were all independent school systems who usually played each other during the season.

Before the Hazard-Paintsville game in the fall of 1946, I was told by Coach Dotson to call Fire Chief Shorty Sizemore at the fire station and ask him if he would sprinkle the field before today's game. It hadn't rained in Hazard in a month and settling the dust would benefit both teams.

I called Chief Sizemore and asked him if he or his crew would wet down the football field for us before game time. He seemed excited to be asked to help and promised to get the job done at least one hour before kickoff.

"We'll do a good job for you," the Chief told me. "You can bet our kids and Paintsville's will have a great field to play on."

Coach Dotson was pleased with the Chief's cooperation to give us a good playing surface for the game. However, what we didn't know was that the Chief had never sprinkled a football field. And because he hadn't he would have to guess at the amount of water needed to dampen the dirt.

A terribly dusty field disappeared when Shorty poured enough water on the ground to float an armada of pontoons. He had messed up royally and what was once a dry playing field now looked like a large farm pond.

One hour before game time the visiting team came to the field to do their warmup drills. When the players and coaches saw the watered down surface, they threw a fit.

Knowing the players would have a tough time playing in regular cleats, my two assistant managers and I rushed to the dressing room with our starting team members. There we changed the regular cleats into mud cleats which were about one inch longer than the ones we removed.

When Coach Dotson heard what had happened at the field he met with the Paintsville coach and assured him that the game would be held up while his players changed to mud cleats.

"Mud cleats hell," the opposing coach responded. "We ain't got no mud cleats with us. We didn't figure we'd need them when we heard that you hadn't had any rain since Noah's day. You ain't heard the last of this."

When the game started the mud was at least two inches over the Paintsville players' shoes. After sloshing through four long quarters of play, Hazard beat Paintsville 50-0. It had been a pushover win for the Hazard team with long cleats against Paintsville's short ones.

As the visiting players and coaches loaded the bus to leave town, the irate coach was heard screaming, "How in the hell do you get a muddy football field when there's been a drought here for a month? It's gotta' be a damn miracle!"

CHAPTER SEVENTEEN

In the summertime Hazard's boys and girls had to create their own entertainment. The city's governing officials made little or no effort to provide recreation facilities for the town's youngsters. There was no swimming pool, no decent baseball field or playgrounds. Funding such projects had to come from the private sector of the town or it didn't come at all.

Daddy and Dennis Sexton had asked the city commission for help buying equipment needed to start a baseball team for teenage boys. Those in charge of the city's pocketbook invariably had excuses as to why they couldn't finance such a program.

So, all of us interested in being on the team had to fend for ourselves. To buy new baseballs, bats and catcher's equipment, we started begging. Listening to our pleas for help (and seeing our sad faces) town merchants began donating to our cause.

We needed at least thirty dollars to buy the equipment sold at Sterling Hardware on Main Street. The money would come from retail stores, filling stations, whiskey stores, or anywhere we thought we might beg for a few dollars.

In search for money I worked Johnson's Ladies Shop and Major's Men's Store. I knew Mrs. Johnson would give in to my sad plea for financial support. She could well afford to give because my mother virtually kept her in business buying the latest frocks from her store. I collected two dollars from her, enough to buy one brand new baseball.

At the end of the day we met at our house on East Main Street and pooled what money we had collected. The total came to forty-three dollars, more than enough to finance a new baseball team. Now all we needed were uniforms which was the same as saying we wanted to buy the Empire State Building. Uniforms were expensive items, too much to finance with our system of collecting money from merchants.

Daddy and Dennis had compiled a rough list of boys who might be interested in becoming a part of the new team. Two weeks into summer vacation we had commitments from eleven boys ages fourteen to sixteen. All we had to do now was to find teams to play in our area and surrounding counties.

The closest teams we could find were in Harlan, Beattyville and Jackson. Playing without uniforms, each of us wore dungarees and white T-shirts. Harlan with superstar Wah Wah Jones had clean white uniforms with large print "HARLAN" on the front of their jerseys. We felt grossly out dressed. Even though we lacked the snazzy appearance of our opponent, we won the game and left Harlan feeling good about our first performance as a new team.

CHAPTER EIGHTEEN

One day when Daddy was doing his weekly banking at the People's Bank he was told by one of the tellers that the bank's president, Finley Case, wanted to talk to him about something or other. When Daddy finished his banking business, he walked a few feet to Mr. Case's office and greeted the president sitting behind his massive walnut desk.

"Good morning, Finley," Daddy greeted as he stepped inside the door. "One of your tellers said you wanted to see me. Hope I haven't over checked my account."

"No no, nothing like that," Finley returned. "Just wanted to talk to you about this new boys' baseball team I've been hearing about. You and Mr. Sexton are to be congratulated for doing something the city government should have done a long time ago."

"We've really had a good time putting this team together. And you wouldn't believe how hard the boys worked to get enough money to buy equipment. I'm really proud of them," Daddy claimed.

"How about uniforms? Do they have any now that they can use?"

"No, Finley, we don't have any kind of outfits to wear other than dungarees and T-shirts. As long as we have the basic equipment to keep us going we'll be okay."

"How many players are on the team?" Finley asked.

"Eleven."

"So you would need at least that many uniforms."

"Yes, that many. However, we don't actually need them at this point in the season," Daddy continued. "But they would certainly be nice to have later on to showcase our boys on the field."

"How much would eleven uniforms cost?" Finley asked.

"I'm not sure, but I know they can be quite expensive."

"Send me the bill when the outfits arrive."

"Do what?"

"Get the bill to me. The bank is going to pay for the twelve uniforms. And we're more than happy to do it."

"I can't believe this," Daddy responded, floored by the offer and leaning forward in his chair. "You're actually going to foot the bill for the boys?"

"Do you have any objections to that?" Finley asked with a smile.

"Are you kidding me? Heck no, I don't have any objection. Why in the world would I? And, uh, by the way, you said twelve uniforms. It's only eleven that we need."

"Are you going to be the manager of the team?"

"Yes I am. Why'd you ask?"

"Because if you are, you should look like a manager, not like some civilian who just stepped off the street. You get the twelfth one."

"My goodness, you're going all the way, aren't you?"

"That's what I've been planning to do. And by the way, do you think Mr. Sexton will want a uniform, too?"

"No, he told me when we started this venture that he had no interest in suiting up for the games."

"Okay, twelve it is. Now you can go get the sizes of the boys and mail your order to whatever company you choose. It'll probably take a while to get the lettering sewed on and get the outfits to you. Again, when they arrive please let me know. Understand?" Finley asked.

"Yes, I do understand, but I'm still shocked in a very nice way about what you're doing. So let me thank you once again before I go and tell the boys the good news. I know all of them will be in hog heaven."

When Daddy called all of us together to tell about Mr. Case's gracious gesture, we couldn't believe what we were hearing. Soon we would be suited up in uniforms that would make us look considerably sharper than when we were dressed in dungarees and T-shirts.

However, we were aware that it was going to take time for the uniforms to be made and shipped to us. No one had any idea when we might see our order come in on the six o'clock train.

CHAPTER NINETEEN

Nearly three weeks after the team meeting with Daddy, Bobby asked Bart and three others if they would like to go camping that night. Of course Bart was always ready to spend time in his favorite environment. Ed Riley, Tom Watson, and Tim Green also agreed to collect their gear and join us for a night in the woods.

At six o'clock we were climbing the steep trail that would eventually lead to our campsite and unfinished cabin. Everything but the roof had been completed on the rugged structure. So instead of sleeping inside a roofless structure we spread our blankets and sleeping bags outside the rough logs.

As soon as we had made our beds Bart started a fire for cooking (frying) our supper. Instead of settling for a downtown take out hamburger, we were looking forward to cooking our own meals in the secluded hills just as our pioneer forefathers had done.

There were no parents, teachers, preachers or any description of grownups telling us what to do or not to do. Our temporary respite from living in town gave us a pleasant touch of euphoria and a welcomed feeling of independence. At least for a while it was our own personal time, our private environment and camaraderie to enjoy without distraction.

For the next thirty minutes I helped Bobby prepare our supper consisting of fried potatoes, bacon, and canned pinto beans. As we cooked on the fire that Bart started the distinct aroma of frying bacon lifted up toward the tall trees surrounding the camp. Somehow it seemed to smell better than when fried at home.

By seven o'clock we had finished our duty as camp chefs and announced, "Okay, come and get it! It's time to eat!" At Bart's call the boys who had been relaxing on grounded beds began gathering their mess kits and canteens. It had taken us about an hour to cook and set up a makeshift buffet line on flat rocks. The food was warm, the campers hungry and the beginning of the end of a summer day perfect for spending time among nature's marvels.

After supper and before darkness set in, Bobby, Bart and I went fifty yards or so away from the camp to practice shooting at empty pinto bean cans. Bobby carried a four- hundred- ten-gauge shotgun and Bart his trusted 30-30-gauge rifle. As a bystander I felt left out of the target practice but I kept my mouth shut.

While we were out on the practice area the rest of the boys were either playing cards, talking about girls or cleaning their mess gear with canteen water. All but Tom were smoking cigarettes that they had taken from their parents' packages earlier in the day. Tom hated the smell of burning tobacco. Made him sniff a lot. But here he had no choice but to smell and bear it.

Three hours later at eleven o'clock the camp was totally quiet except for the nighttime creatures that had begun throwing out their nocturnal voices. No moon lit the partially clouded sky, and wild dogs could be faintly heard howling on the ridge above us.

No movement in the camp.

Light snoring and gas passings were in the air (fueled by Bobby's pinto beans).

Suddenly, without warning the loud blast of a high powered rifle broke through the quiet of the dark night. POW! POW! POW! POW!

The deafening sound of four exploding bullets at close range rang out over our heads. In a flash I was petrified from the blast that sounded so close to the camp. By instinct, I guess, I crawled ten feet or so and found safety crowding against a log wall inside the cabin. Others followed my lead. In a few seconds all but Bart had made it to the safety spot I'd found.

I could barely see him getting out of his bedding with the 30-30 rifle in his hand. It was still loaded from the target shooting he practiced just before dark. Suddenly as fast as he could cock the rifle he retaliated with three shots.

POW! POW! POW! Aimed in the direction of the loud blasts from the mysterious visitor's gun.

When the echo of the rifle began fading, a loud voice rang out from the area of the first gunfire.

"HOLD IT DAMN IT HOLD IT!" it pleaded. "DON'T SHOOT AGAIN! IT'S ME, CRAWFORD!"

Crawford.

Crawford Roberts.

The centerfielder on our baseball team.

One who nearly had his brains extracted by Bart's bullets.

In quick step Crawford made his way into the camping area while all of us inside the cabin came out of our fort of safety. Everyone in the camp knew that our unexpected visitor was about to catch hell from Bart and the others. His senseless actions had scared the wits out of all except Bart. He was shooting to kill and Crawford let him know how close he came to doing it.

"The leaves above my head were moving because of your shots," the latecomer claimed. "I really thought I was going to get my butt shot off."

"I should have aimed lower you sonofabitch," Bart returned with a scowl. "Why in the hell did you do such a thing? You know better than to use a gun to scare people."

"I know. I know," Crawford returned now embarrassed by his stunt. "I couldn't get here any earlier so I thought I'd have a little fun while you guys were asleep."

"A little fun, eh?" Bobby shot back. "Your idea of fun might have gotten somebody killed. You know that, don't you?"

"Nah, nobody was goin' to get hurt. Heck, I aimed at least ten feet above your heads." Crawford returned. "Now I think I can make all of you feel a lot better with some good news I've brought with me."

"What kind of news?" Bobby asked. "If you have some then let us hear it. After what you did to us it better be good."

"Okay, here it is," Crawford began. "Guess what, the uniforms are in. They came on the train tonight."

"Are you bullin' with us just to get your butt off the hot seat? Repeat what you just said," Bart replied skeptically.

"I swear it's true. The uniforms came tonight. Asher has them in his basement and he wants all of us to be at his house at ten o'clock tomorrow morning to try them on."

Frowns and scowls that had been thrown at Crawford when he appeared suddenly turned into little smiles. After all the days of waiting, our uniforms were now only one hour away from us. And because of the good news he brought, we slowly began forgiving our centerfielder for his alarming arrival at the camp.

It took a while for us to settle down and try to get some sleep before the night was gone. Crawford's loud arrival and the great news about the uniforms probably kept adrenalin flowing high in all of us.

Shortly after midnight the area gradually became quiet again. Nothing was moving. Nobody was talking. Only the creatures of the night were communicating with each other. They were probably wondering what the heck has been going on with the weird creatures lying on the ground below them.

At 5:30 A.M. daybreak did an encore. The arrival of first light revealed blankets heavily dampened by the dew of the night. The air was uncomfortably cool and all of us struggled to find a hint of warmth inside our bedding. One hour later the first sign of life appeared. I came from under my covers and began a slow, unsteady gait toward the side of the cabin. Nature had made its first call of the day and I was on my way to answer it.

As I was doing my business, I glanced up through the light fog above me and wondered, "Why do men always look up when they're emptying their bladders?" They do, but what's up there to see? I've never found a single thing above my head worth looking at. "Hmmmmmmm," I quietly groaned finishing my call from nature. "That's really a nutty thought."

Seven o'clock brought more life to the camp. Bart was first to get out of his bedding and make an effort to start another fire. Ashes left from the night before felt cold and damp. He also felt chilled and tired from having a restless night of sleep.

But now it was time for the boys to get back into the world of living. "EVERYBODY GET UP!" Bart shouted. "After the fire is goin' there ain't goin' be nobody sackin' out! Stayin' in bed too long is goin' to get cold water poured on your face!"

"Aw, pipe down," a disgusted voice came from under Tom's covers.

"We don't have a train to catch or a class to go to so please quit hollering your brains out."

"Ah, but we do have a deadline to meet," Bart returned. "Do you remember where we're supposed to be at ten o'clock?"

"Yeah, yeah, yeah," Tom returned. "I know where we're supposed to be. But for now please put a sock in your mouth. It's only a little after seven."

Bart's loud commands had shaken us out of our final attempts to grab more winks. Movement was slow. But in a few minutes each of us was standing and stretching away the stiffness the hard ground had sunk into our bodies. Bobby added to Bart's orders.

"It's after seven right now and we have a lot to do today. So get those blankets together and put your butts in gear."

Hot coffee and stale bakery doughnuts made up the morning menu. We huddled around the fire and each other as we gulped down the pastry and caffeine. Our energy soon began making a slow return to our bodies with the appearance of the warm morning sun. Best of all, the promise made to us four weeks earlier had reached fruition— the uniforms were here.

CHAPTER TWENTY

Before leaving camp we finished packing our bedding, put out the fire and made certain nothing of value was left behind. Once our chores were completed we left the area in single file.

Forty five minutes later we reached our house where Mother met and directed us straightway to the basement. Once there, we found the other members of the team trying on their uniforms.

"Well lookee here," Ed Riley greeted us dingy looking campers. "Looks like all of you have been run through a tough wringer. But I'll tell you what, here's somethin' that'll perk you up a little. I guarantee it."

After offering his guarantee, Ed tossed his jersey to Bobby. "Take a look at that ol' buddy," he said as Bobby caught the top half of the uniform. "Ain't that somethin' special?"

And special it was.

Bobby's eyes squinted for a moment then opened wide as he looked at the large red letters sewed across the gray jersey spelling "HAZARD" Twelve spanking new outfits. All first class. Over the next few minutes Daddy passed out uniforms to the rest of the campers. I had been staring in awe at the professional looking outfits the likes of which none of us had ever seen.

The only player who seemed to be in a distraught mindset was me. I couldn't have felt worse as I slipped out of my camping clothes and put on a uniform that was at least three sizes too big for me. The bottom of the pants covered my shoes. The name "HAZARD" with letters that should have covered by upper chest was almost under my waistline. And the baseball cap was so large that the brim nearly came down over my eyes.

For the youngest of the group my last few minutes had been a total disaster. Then to make the awkward scene even worse some of the boys began laughing at me when they saw my major misfits.

Embarrassed to the bone, I couldn't keep from crying while pulling up my pants to keep them from falling to the floor. Without a doubt I was going through one of the worst moments of my life.

Bobby and Bart couldn't help but see the situation I was in. Bobby responded to the laughter with an intimidating look and authoritative voice.

"Quit laughing at my brother right now or I'm goin' to start kicking some butts!" he warned.

"Yeah, that goes for me too," Bart backed Bobby's order. "You damned guys ought to be ashamed of yourselves. Just because he's small and got a big fit doesn't give you the right to make fun of him. So all of you back off. He's still one of us small or not!"

When Bart spoke the laughter began to fade.

Daddy had watched the tense scene long enough. He knew he had to do something to make me believe that the uniform problem was going to be solved. He walked to me, put his arm around my shoulder and said, "You know, son, your mother can work on that uniform and make it fit like a big leaguer's outfit. You know that don't you?"

I nodded yes to Daddy then without speaking wiped my eyes and broke a big smile at him. "Do you really think Mother can fix all of this? It's sure goin' to take a lot of cuttin' and sewin' to bring it down to my size."

"Son, don't worry about it," Daddy returned. "You're goin' to have the best fittin' uniform on the team. Believe me."

"If I was a little bigger I'd knock the snot out of every one of 'em who laughed at me." I said to Daddy. "It wasn't funny. Not one bit."

CHAPTER TWENTY-ONE

With our spiffy look in the new uniforms we were anxious to play our first game in front of our local fans. They would be watching a game being played on a rocky football field poorly transformed into a baseball diamond. It was the only field we had to play on and it was a real doozy.

Since there was no flat ground in right field the fielder had to stand on an angled slope to play his position. Ruts made from years of erosion were deep enough to bury a pregnant opossum. And the grass that wasn't on the football field wasn't in right field either. This section of the field could justifiably be called a topographical abortion.

Centerfield was okay. It was flat because it was in the middle of the football field with no ruts or steep slopes. Without a doubt this field was the last place on earth that any team would want to play baseball. But our players had no choice. We were forced to deal with all the negative features of the playing area we faced in practice and each game. But with our new uniforms we were too excited to worry about a bad baseball field.

Against a good Jenkins team Bobby pitched a two hit shutout and hit a homerun his second time at bat. We won the game 7-0. What a great day it had been with the victory coming in front of our hometown fans and to feel proud to look like a young professional team.

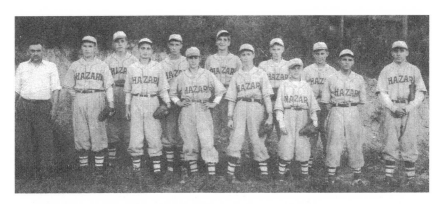

Hazard boys' baseball team in new uniforms

Six games later our baseball season ended. Out of the six we won five then put away our equipment for the year. It was good to know that when next spring comes around we will once again proudly step into our uniforms and begin playing a brand new season.

CHAPTER TWENTY-TWO

In my freshman year I quit taking piano lessons. Mother finally gave up on me. I thought I had convinced her that I wasn't going to be a famous piano artist when I forgot my recital piece four years earlier. I shouted for joy when I found myself free on Thursdays.

In the eleventh grade I was playing basketball in a Hazard High blue and gold uniform that gave me a lot of pride to wear. The team I was on was only so-so for we were young and having problems playing against veteran teams. But we were learning. By the end of the season we had become a comparatively good squad and looked forward to the next season when our maturity would undoubtedly be a huge asset.

I finished the season winning small gold basketballs for making the all-district and all-regional teams. By the end of my junior year I had become a pretty good basketball player.

One major drawback for Hazard High players was the unbelievable gymnasium where the home games were played. The playing court was small compared to regulation size gymnasiums found in a few schools in the mountains.

The ceiling was low and angled because of the slanted floor in the auditorium directly above the gymnasium. Visiting teams rarely adjusted to this negative feature, often hitting the ceiling with their shots that were automatically called out of bounds.

Throwing the ball inbounds meant standing on fans' shoes resting on the out of bounds line that went all around the court.

Considering all its negative features, Hazard High's gym should have been condemned for public use. It was the worst feature in the original floor plan of the high school built in 1926.

CHAPTER TWENTY-THREE

New boy and girl in town!! In a small town that's news. Jimmy Bergman moved to Hazard from Cincinnati and Phyllis Rollins pulled up stakes in Harlan, Kentucky and came to Perry County.

There was always a mysterious air around new folks who came to settle in our town. Who are they? Why did they come here? Think the new boy plays sports? The girl's pretty. Wonder if she'll go out on a date?

It took only a few days to discover that the new ones didn't come from Mars. They were just like we were and in a few short days we forgot the "new" label that we put on them.

Jimmy Bergman, the one from Cincinnati, was two years ahead of me in school. Despite the age difference we clicked like long lost brothers. The reason we meshed was simple— music. When we discovered that each of us loved the same kind of songs, we sang anywhere and everywhere.

In my sophomore year and Jimmy's senior year we entered the Hazard High amateur contest as the Risner brothers. Jimmy had to con Bobby Ross into playing the guitar for us because Bobby was a devout member of the Church of God and his denomination frowned on playing or singing secular music. But Jimmy, the master persuader, talked Bobby into joining us.

Wearing coonskin hats, overalls, red plaid shirts and brogan boots we sang our tails off and won the high school contest. By winning there we became eligible to enter the countywide competition scheduled to take place in ten days.

Before the event we practiced once or twice singing old mountain standards "The Maple on the Hill", "Smoke on the Water", and "The Old Country Church". I sang tenor high enough to break glass twenty-feet away. My voice hadn't changed so we could pitch tunes much higher than what a mature voice could handle.

The big night came and we were ready. The contestants ahead of us did their things while we warmed up outside the back door. Bobby was a fine guitarist and since we were having so much fun in the competition, he forgot about the taboo his church placed on worldly music.

When the call came for us to go on stage we walked on singing "The Maple on the Hill" and got heavy applause from Hazard High friends in the audience. After the second tune we did a short comedy routine with Jimmy saying:

"Hey, Don, Bobby, lookee here, I done gone and larned how to write somethin'. Yeah, I shore have."

Don: "You've learned to write? Is that what you're sayin'?"

Jimmy: "Yep. Larned how to yesterday."

Bobby: "Well, if you've larned how to write, what does it say?"

Jimmy: "Uh, don't rightly know, ain't learned to read yet."

We won the contest hands down. It was an amateur contest but for some reason we were paid five silver dollars for winning. Bobby spent his on the way home. Jimmy and I still have ours.

That night, for the first time, I was paid for singing on stage. I liked it. Jimmy and I sang together for two years at parties or any sort of get -together where there was a piano. We even did a radio show or two before he left for Centre College in the Fall of 1947.

I missed my best friend. I missed our singing and being together. With him I was introduced to performing in front of a crowd without becoming a nervous wreck. I liked that, too. Jimmy Bergman was an important figure in my life.

After graduating from Centre, Jimmy joined the U.S. Navy for a three year tour of duty. We stayed in touch but with him being assigned to a base in Japan I knew it would be a good while before we saw each other again.

When I think back to the times when Jimmy and I were in high school I can still see him, Daddy, my brother and me sitting on our screened in porch on a warm summer night singing old close harmony songs. The chords weren't perfect but it didn't matter.

CHAPTER TWENTY-FOUR

During my last year as equipment manager I was pleased to find that we were to play Frankfort High School in football in an away game. In late October Frankfort was ranked the number one football team in Kentucky.

Our coach, Ed Dotson, a Frankfort native, wanted the chance to dethrone the Frankfort High team from its lofty ranking. Doing that he could show his old hometown friends what a fine team he had developed in Hazard.

On the bus trip to Frankfort the team members, coaches and I had the opportunity to travel through the beauty of Central Kentucky. There we saw the famous thoroughbred horse farms and miles and miles of beautiful rolling land where champion stallions and mares graze. We also had the opportunity to see our state's capitol building for the first time.

I had been to Frankfort several times with my parents but this trip was different. I felt a sense of freedom and pride being in charge of all the equipment that our team needed to perform. In that category, I was the boss.

Once at the hotel the team members and I were given assigned rooms followed by a pre-game meal in the hotel dining room. Some of Coach Dotson's Frankfort friends stopped by the hotel and visited with their old buddy for a few minutes.

In their conversation one of the coach's visitors gave him a quick evaluation of the team he would be facing that night. His parting words were, "You best be on your toes during the game. Our boys are proud of their high ranking and they don't plan on losing to anybody. They'll try to hit you hard so be ready."

Two hours later we faced a team determined not to let the boys from Hazard or anywhere else take away their star status.

At the start of the game we were in trouble. When Bobby sent the opening kick to the five yard line, the Frankfort receiver didn't stop until Kern Walls tackled him after a fifty-yard run.

The Frankfort team blocked exceptionally well for its kickoff returner. So well that three Hazard players were lying down and out on the ground. Those prostrate youngsters had become victims of vicious blocking by the Frankfort kickoff return team.

Before the next play two helpers and I ran onto the field to tend to the injured players. One by one we carried the dazed boys to the Hazard bench area and dropped them to the ground. One play. Three players already down. And Coach Dotson feared that things might get worse in the four quarters yet to be played.

The game wore on through three devastating periods for the Hazard eleven. By the start of the final quarter my helpers and I carried two more injured players from the playing field to our bench. Now the coach was forced to play second and third stringers and the game was ten minutes from being over.

To add to the misery of the night, Dick Thomas, our two- hundred-thirty pound tackle came to the bench with an unexpected announcement: his jockey strap broke and it was the only one we had that would fit him.

"My pecker's hangin'," he informed Coach Dotson. "The jock's nearly down to my knees."

Hearing that admission, Coach turned to me and said, "Well, don't just stand there get him another one. You're the equipment manager aren't you?"

"We don't have another one, Coach," I informed. "But maybe I can fix the one he's wearin'."

"Well do it fast. The timeout's gonna' be over in another minute or so."

"Oh boy, this ain't gonna' be easy," I thought quickly. "Not easy at all." But somewhere in the ad lib section of my brain I guess it hit me that I was going to have to try and tie two torn ends of the strap together. Thinking that it just might work I called four substitutes over and told them to form a circle around Dick and me while Dick dropped his pants.

"Hurry up!" I called frantically. "We have to get him back in the game before it's over or Coach Dotson is gonna' kill me."

Four willing substitutes hustled to make a fairly large circle around Dick and me and I immediately began trying to tie this huge strap back together. Pulling as hard as I could, I stretched the two ends even then twisted them into a knot about the same size as a small fist. Voile! It was holding together but I think Dick's eyes were bulging from the tightness of the restructured strap. We finished our challenging project in time for Dick to rush back to his team now in a huddle.

I'll never forget the sight of a huge young man trotting back onto the playing field with a knot on his side that looked like a large tumor. Fortunately for Dick the strap held for the rest of the game and mercifully we escaped the 28-0 slaughter at Frankfort High School without seeing more serious injuries.

I felt certain that this would be the last time to schedule a team that's ranked as the best in the state. But if it wasn't, I would make certain that we bought a stretcher to make it easier to carry our wounded off the playing field. And most importantly, we would buy an extra jockey strap for Dick Thomas.

CHAPTER TWENTY-FIVE

My brother Bobby who survived the Frankfort game was blessed with as much athletic ability as any player who ever attended Hazard High. He was a first team all-state basketball player, an all-conference football player two years in a row and pitched baseball never losing a game in his high school or college careers. He once entered six events in a track meet and won all six.

He received a letter from Coach Bear Bryant asking him to visit the University of Kentucky campus and consider coming out for his team. Bobby politely replied to the letter informing Mr. Bryant that his interest was in basketball and that he would probably be attending Vanderbilt.

While I was slow growing in my physical maturity, Bobby looked like a grownup when he was in the tenth grade. He was six feet tall, well built and full of that intangible trait called "character".

Once when Coach Dotson's football team had a less than perfect practice session, he demanded that the entire team run five laps around the perimeter of the football field. I was still the equipment manager at the time and was responsible for opening and closing the main door before and after practice.

When the exhausted players who ran the laps came to the dressing room to shower and change clothes I failed to notice that Bobby wasn't with them. In thirty minutes or so the room was empty but Bobby's clothes were still hanging on his metal hook.

Just as darkness was beginning to move in I looked out the back door and saw a silhouette of a player still running laps. It had to be Bobby. He

65

was the only player left who hadn't changed clothes. When he finally came to the room to shower and dress I asked him how many laps he'd run and to my question he answered twenty.

Twenty times. In the darkness. Nobody saw him doing it. Later he told me that he hadn't given his best effort in practice and needed to get in better shape to be a better player.

Character—that was one of my brother's strengths.

CHAPTER TWENTY-SIX

In the fall of 1948 I entered my senior year loaded with expectations regarding the upcoming basketball season. I was honored to have been picked by local newspapers as the one most likely to be the best player in our region and one of the better players in Eastern Kentucky. Of course that meant that the pressure of living up to that forecast was going to be rather heavy. But I was ready to take on the challenge and my teammates were just as anxious and prepared as I to get the season underway.

And then there were girls. Yeah boy, lots of them. The boys had three choices: go steady, play the field or spend time wishing for either of the first two.

I knew I was going to like dating. It really started in my junior year when I asked a gorgeous young lady to be my date to the spring dance. Sally Reynolds was the shyest person I had ever met. If you spoke to her she would blush. If you didn't speak to her she would blush.

Sally sat behind me in a general business class and said nothing unless called on by the teacher. After about one month I finally got her to open up a bit about the weather, a particular teacher, movies or some other topic.

I think Sally got the shock of her young life when I, the great and glorious basketball star asked her to be my date for the Key Club dance.

She was totally stunned, not from being impressed by the invitation but by the fact that she thought she wasn't good enough to go with me. She blushed four different shades and finally said, "You really don't want me for a date, do you?" To which I replied, "I want you and nobody else to go to that dance with me in two weeks. Tell me you'll be my date."

I really didn't think she would accept my invitation, but then to my surprise she opened up and asked more questions than I thought she had in her. In little more than a whisper she finally said, "Thanks for asking me. I want to go with you."

The big night finally came and I in my white dinner jacket, black tie and cummberbund drove our 1948 Ford to Eversole Street to pick up Sally. Her mother met me at the door, introduced herself and asked me to have a seat while she checked to see if Sally was ready to go.

Sally was ready all right. She came out of her bedroom looking much like a Hollywood movie star. I think I swallowed my tongue twice. She was absolutely gorgeous in a light blue velvet top matched with a floor length dark skirt.

I complimented her on her appearance and as expected she blushed and asked in a timid voice, "Do I look okay to you? Is this outfit all right?"

I could have told her that she looked like Elizabeth Taylor but I doubt if she would had believed me. I don't think I had ever seen a more beautiful young lady in my life.

At the dance she was quiet and obviously unsure of herself around the other girls her age. To me she was the queen of the ball. No other girl came close to being as pretty as little Molly.

When I took her home after the dance we got into that awkward moment on her front porch of to kiss or not to kiss. I was shocked to the bottom of my patent leather shoes when without warning she stepped close to me and kissed me lightly on the lips. I think she was trying to say, "Thank you, I had a good time." If that was what she was thinking I admit that she made her point. It had been a good night for both of us.

I didn't date Sally again after our first outing. I don't know exactly why except maybe Miss Carolyn Webb (another Miss America in our midst) had attracted my attention. But Sally and I remained friends. I think maybe our date helped break down the barrier that had kept her at arm's length from boys her age.

CHAPTER TWENTY-SEVEN

Vocal music became important to me when I reached high school. I had been singing in the junior choir at our Baptist church since I was in the seventh grade. What I discovered about my music was that practically no age is too young to begin enjoying it.

I sang tenor with my dad when I was ten years old. I had no idea why I could do it and became even more amazed when out of the blue I started singing bass with no training whatsoever.

Everyone in my family was blessed with the talent of singing various parts of a song. My dad sang solos in church, Mother was an alto in the church choir and brother Bobby sang baritone with me in the junior choir.

I remember many Sunday nights after church we would stop at the drugstore, order four cokes to go and ride around for an hour or so singing harmony. The acoustics in a car are perfect because chords don't have anywhere to go except to the front and back of the interior and then bounce back off the headliner.

Those were special nights to remember. The four of us were together enjoying the solid harmony, never dreaming that someday this scene would be gone with time. I guess we thought our harmonizing would go on forever.

Later I sang with a quartet with three guys who loved to sing as much as I did. We performed at all three civic clubs in town and did a decent job of entertaining the members. I really didn't think we were very good but do admit that we had a lot of guts.

That same year our foursome sang in a statewide contest for public schools. We didn't do so hot. If memory serves me correctly I think we came in last against all the other quartets.

CHAPTER TWENTY-EIGHT

In late October the basketball season started for all schools in Kentucky. At the same time last year all ten of us on the team were like lambs being taken to the proverbial slaughter. We had no experience. None. And we showed it by having a bad season.

But that was all behind us. Twenty-five games the previous year had given us a world of confidence and experience. Now we were ready to fire our best shots at the competition.

We played fairly well during the first part of the season but things got tougher when we got into the meat of our schedule.

In a Christmas tournament in Winchester, we won our first game defeating Cynthiana High by a good margin. We lost the second one to Eminence High School but I was fortunate in being chosen on the all-tournament team consisting of only five players. Future University of Kentucky star Cliff Hagan was also one of the five.

1948

Owensboro star Cliff Hagan has 23 points, but the Red Devils are upset by Eminence 39-37 in the Winchester Invitational. Owensboro led 37-31 and went to a stall, but the strategy backfired. Hagan, Bob Mulcahy of Lafayette, Don McGuire of Hazard, Harvey Hackworth of Madison Central and J.W. Johnson of Eminence are on the all-tournament team. ... Dwight Price's 8-foot shot in the final seconds gives U-High a 40-39 win over Shelbyville in the Kiwanis Invitational final at UK's Alumni Gym.

At the end of the regular season we had won eighteen games and lost five. Not bad, but we had expected to do much better. The opportunity to improve our overall record was coming in the district and regional tournaments. With the experience we gained in the regular season we were primed to give the competition a tough run. And we did.

Two victories in the district tournament gave us the championship and eventually put us in the final regional game against a good team from Hindman High School. One more victory and we would be heading for the state tournament in Louisville.

The game was close until the middle of the third quarter. That's when we broke it open when I hit three consecutive long shots to put us ahead by six points. John Green, our other guard, hit two more behind mine and suddenly we were on our way to a kill. We won the game by twenty-one points.

A dramatic scene occurred with my grandfather, Sam Combs, who lived deep in the hills of Eastern Kentucky. He had never seen me play in a basketball game but kept track of our season on his little battery operated radio.

When he heard me hit the three tie breaking shots against Hindman in the third quarter, he walked out to the front porch and jubilantly fired his twelve gauge shotgun three times into the darkness in front of him. For my grandfather and all Hazard Bulldog fans it was indeed a special night.

CHAPTER TWENTY-NINE

In the state high school tournament we were scared playing in front of seven thousand fans. That's a few hundred more than the population of Hazard. I'd never seen that many people under one roof.

Our game was against a good Lafayette High team out of Lexington. From start to finish of the first half we played like a bunch of nitwits. In the second half four of us managed to get the large crowd off our minds and play some decent basketball. Not so for Phil Warden. He was a nervous wreck warming up and stayed that way the entire game.

Strangely, he hummed the same song from the game's start to finish. Once when he passed the ball to me and ran by my side I could hear Mmmmmmmm (that's a hum). He finally stopped humming when the final horn sounded. Phil didn't score a point.

We lost the game by thirteen points and Lafayette went on to be the runner-up

Competition said I had springs in my legs.

73

in the tournament. We had wanted to make a much better showing in the big city but it just didn't happen. At least we made it to the tournament along with fifteen other schools.

When I looked back to the past season and thought of my teammates I found it gratifying to know that the starting five on our team had all set goals to further their education. We were all college bound: John Green to Centre College, Timmy Brown to the University of Kentucky, Ray Greer and I to Western Kentucky and Phil Warden (the hummer) to Eastern Kentucky. Our teachers and administrators were aware of our goals and let each of us know they were proud of our intentions.

One month after basketball season ended our baseball team began its season. This spring sport really didn't bring much excitement to the students. It was the slowest of all the high school sports. Consequently, the stands weren't running over with spectators. The players weren't too choked up about it either. But at least it gave us something to do until school was out.

I pitched and played second base for two seasons. With my size most opposing batters surmised that I would not be a fastball pitcher. But I was and it fooled them so much that I struck out sixteen batters on the Prestonsburg High team in a regular season game.

When the district tournament began in late May, I was chosen to pitch the final game. Leslie County had a fairly good team with the Martin brothers being the stars. When each one came to bat I would try to throw my best pitches which were the knuckle ball and the side arm curve.

Both pitches worked just fine until Mack Moseley hit one into centerfield looking to be a surefire two bagger. But on a dead run our centerfielder, Al Salley, made a diving catch for the third out.

Through six and one-half innings the score stood at 1-0 in our favor. All we had to do was get through one more one-half inning and we would be district champions.

Before beginning the bottom of the seventh inning, Coach Osborne came to the mound to give me encouragement when facing the next Leslie County hitters. As he began turning to go back to the dugout he looked at me squarely in the eyes and said, "You know you have a no hitter going, don't you?"

Stunned by his information, I gulped once or twice and replied, "No, I didn't know it, Coach. Why in the devil did you have to tell me now?"

"Sorry," Coach Osborne said. "I thought your knowing would make you bear down a little more. Just get'em out and let's go home," Coach finished the conversation.

Bearing down, I struck out the next two hitters with my knuckleball then looked toward the visitor's dugout to see who their next batter would be. I should have guessed it. It was Dan Moseley, their heaviest hitter. And I had to get him out to get this game in our win column.

Moseley was a big man, probably six-feet-four, weighing well over two hundred pounds. He knew that he represented the tying run and would undoubtedly be swinging for the fences.

"What pitch should I throw him?" I thought quickly. Fastball? No, he'd be waiting for that one. Curve? No, he's a good curveball hitter. I finally decided to pitch a change-up to him knowing he was so fired up he might over swing on a slow pitch. We stared each other down for a few seconds before I went into my windup. The pitch I threw was so slow that I doubted for a second if the ball would make it to the plate. It did make it and Moseley swung hard only to hit a harmless pop up in foul territory over third base.

Our fielder waited for what seemed to be an eternity for the ball to come down, aimed his glove up at it and made the catch that would send us to the regional tournament.

The team was ecstatic. All the players were jumping up and down, hugging each other while yelling to the top of their collective voice, "We done gone and done it!! Yeah, the Bulldogs have done it!!!"

When the celebrating was nearly over, Charles Hill, the Hazard scorekeeper came out of the dugout and in a loud voice announced to the team, "Don has just thrown a no-hitter. No hits. Not a one."

Cheers went up for me. I honestly didn't realize that I was in the position of throwing a no-hitter until Coach Osborne came to the mound and told me.

A no-hitter! WOW!! I got lucky.

CHAPTER THIRTY

The baseball season ended in late April with us losing to Lee County in the first game of the regional tournament. Now we were looking at six weeks before school was out and I would soon be graduating.

Soon after our season was over Mrs. Emma Ross, our tough English teacher, stopped me in the first floor hallway and informed me that she had chosen me to be the male lead in the final play of the year. I thought I'd choke trying to think of a way to talk her out of giving me the part. But she seemed dead-set on having me in her production.

Still not giving up, I offered a lame excuse as to why I wasn't available to be a part of her cast.

"Mrs. Ross, I really don't think that I can do what you're asking. My dad is counting on me to help him with a lot of chores around the house and I don't think…"

"Don, let me stop you looking for an excuse," Mrs. Ross jumped in. "Your senior English grades are sort of borderline and I think in your best interest you should consider that they could go lower."

I hushed, looked down at the floor for a second thinking of my grades in her class. They weren't so hot. My next remark to her put me in show business.

"When do we start rehearsing?"

Mrs. Ross answered my question, informing that rehearsal on the first scene would begin in three days.

After beginning practice I realized that our play, "Shiny Nose" was no potential Academy Award winner. But Mrs. Ross believed it was good enough to entertain an audience for ninety minutes.

Carolyn Webb played my wife in the play. I thought she was the prettiest girl in our class and few disagreed with me. I had no idea that I would ever have a romantic interest in her. She had been dating Bobby Allen and I assumed that their relationship was still on solid ground. But being together for three weeks of rehearsing gave our biological juices a chance to mingle and a mutual attraction gradually emerged.

On weekends Carolyn and I doubled dated with Paul Toms and Alice Higgs. It was a great time to be nineteen years old. High school was nearly finished after which would come a few weeks of free time until we made final decisions on which colleges we might attend.

Worries were something that grownups had to deal with while our most pressing concern was trying to decide what to wear on tonight's date. These might well have been some of the happiest days we would ever see in our lives. At the time, however, we never gave it a thought. Maudlin? Perhaps. But okay.

And then, of course, there were those special times when Carolyn and I would find a suitable parking place to discuss the problems of the world (uh huh). We knew that Hitler lost so what else was there to do but to give each other some victory rewards.

The night for the presentation of the senior play finally made it and we were set to give it our best shot. Lois Lusk played the comedy part to perfection and I was the wise and lovable father. I think Mrs. Ross was pleased with my performance. She must have been because my grade standing in her room didn't drop.

CHAPTER THIRTY-ONE

Summer 1949

After graduating in May, spring and early summer held some of the more exciting days of my life. Just when I thought I would choose a college by late April my decision was put on hold. I received an invitation from Coach Ed Diddle of Western Kentucky State College to play in the Kentucky-Indiana High School All-star game in Indianapolis. This was a big deal for me and probably for the other eleven players chosen from across the state.

To get to Bowling Green Daddy let me drive one of our two cars. I would make the trip with no one in the car but me. No backseat drivers. No one telling long, boring stories. Just me. What a great feeling it was to be independent and to have what could be exciting days ahead! The miles seemed to zip by. And once I found my way to the Western campus I felt proud that I had successfully made the trip without incident. My next stop was at Coach Diddle's office in the gymnasium.

When I met Mr. Diddle I was impressed with his friendly smile and what seemed to be a genuine interest in who I was and where I was from. While chatting with him I thought, "I'm talking to a college coach who's famous for producing championship teams."

Just a few weeks earlier he and his squad had been in New York and Philadelphia where they won two games against tough competition. Now he was volunteering his time and coaching talents to work with one dozen high school players from McDowell in far Eastern Kentucky to Paducah in the West.

While in his office I met some of the players I would be living with plus one of Coach Diddle's starting forwards on the Western team. He was tall, slender, handsome and friendly. I was impressed with the way he spoke to everyone around him.

Western's gym was just outside the coach's door and I could see immediately that this was no dinky high school basketball court. It looked big time with wide stripes instead of one small paint strip marking the out of bounds lines. Birds chirped in the space near the high ceiling and the radio announcer's booth was large enough to hold a dozen people. The booth at our home gym barely had enough space to seat a large dog.

From Coach Diddle's office we were taken to where we would be living until leaving for Indianapolis. Oddly, the Western varsity players lived in the backside of the Diddle home. Only one door separated the players from his family's living area. There's where we would be staying with the Western squad members who were going to summer school.

In the Diddle home, where I met the other players, I would be with the next ten days or so. The big star, Frank Ramsey, had already signed to play with the University of Kentucky. He was projected to be our star of stars in the upcoming game. If he played to the top of his ability we would be running and gunning with a player loaded with talent.

Bill "Wild Bill" Stumbo from McDowell High School turned out to be one of the toughest players on the squad to guard. He was deceptively quick making it virtually impossible to tell which way he was going to throw the ball or if he would run to the left or right when he took off. Bill also had a wonderful sense of humor using his Eastern Kentucky twang to make conversation colorful.

One of the more interesting players to talk to was Mason Cooke of tiny Brewers High School in Marshall County. His school had only one hundred students in grades seven through twelve and less than one-half that number were boys. In that tiny high school ten of the boys were exceptionally good basketball players. When the 1948 State Championship trophy was handed to the team, Brewers became the first high school squad in Kentucky basketball history to go undefeated the entire season. That record is still standing one-half century later.

Mason was friendly enough but a bit cocky. He seemed to still be gloating over the huge success his small school had recorded during the 1947-1948 season.

Gradually, all twelve members of our team came to know each other as the days of hot practice sessions moved on. I can remember the humid summer nights when most of the team would visit the College Street Inn for footlong hot dogs and huge slices of watermelon as desserts. At the time, songs "Again" and "The Tennessee Waltz" were the tunes played most on juke boxes and radios around town.

Those were happy and carefree times. Very little was on our minds except the upcoming game against the Hoosier team. Well, maybe our thoughts turned toward home and the sweet things we had to leave behind for a few days. I know I missed seeing Carolyn every night but our separation was only for a few days. I could stand that.

I think our entire team was impressed with Western's varsity players we were living with in the Diddle home. They looked more mature than we did. They talked about courses they were taking that had strange names like kinesiology, physiology, mammalian anatomy and other esoteric titles we'd never heard of. This was college talk but with basketball on our minds we couldn't care less about their sophisticated courses.

After five days of hot and tough practices the team was beginning to come together. Frank Ramsey lived up to his reputation of being a talented basketball star. The rest of the players showed the skills that got them on what we believed to be an outstanding high school All Star team.

Time to leave for Indianapolis finally came. Coach Diddle asked me if I would take four players in my car and join the other two vehicles for the trip. I agreed of course with the assurance that I would be reimbursed for what I spent on gasoline.

We left Bowling Green at nine o'clock Friday morning driving, about four hours to the site of our game. Once there we checked into the hotel, unpacked our bags then headed for Butler Fieldhouse where we would have our final practice before Saturday's game.

The place was huge. It seated over twelve thousand fans, making it twice the size of my hometown. Worst of all, there would be approximately twelve thousand Indiana rooters and maybe if we're lucky one hundred Kentucky followers yelling for us. Needless to say, we were going to be grossly outnumbered.

Following a light practice we went back to the hotel and took a short rest before going to a special dinner given for both teams. It probably wasn't going to be easy sitting across the table from the player you were going to guard within the next twenty-four hours. Maybe the Indiana boys felt the same way. I'd guess they would since they were no older or probably no more mature than we were.

Awkwardly we talked to each other, faked our laughs and acted as if we were long lost relatives. At the time I wasn't interested in being an uncle. I was already trying to figure how to beat my man if we got into a one-on-one situation.

Coach Diddle told me in advance which player I would guard if I went into the game. His name was Ron White from Muncie, Indiana and was reputed to be a guard with great speed. His one shortcoming was that he was only five-feet-eight inches tall, two and one-half inches shorter than I. Regardless of his size I was concerned about staying with him when he turned on his speed.

Ron White was probably a fine fellow, but at the moment I didn't give a hoot about his personality and character. I'd think about that later.

CHAPTER THIRTY-TWO

The day of the game finally arrived and we were ready to put into motion what we'd been practicing for the past week. At 5:30 we loaded the cars and headed for Butler Fieldhouse, planning to arrive there around ninety minutes before game time.

On the way very little was said. Nerves were undoubtedly beginning to get a bit shaky but whatever tension we might have had seemed under control.

By the time we got to the dressing room and began putting on our uniforms I couldn't help but think of playing in front of thousands of people all against us. But to negate that thought I began thinking about the amount of pride I was going to feel wearing the game jersey with the letters K-E-N-T-U-C-K-Y sewn across the front. The large stars below the letters spoke a silent message to me, " Tonight you are representing every high school basketball player in the state of Kentucky. Wear the uniform with a great deal of pride."

During our warmup I noticed some of the differences between high school and college gyms. Here you could smell popcorn popping, see extra large scoreboards in the fieldhouse as opposed to our small oval shaped ones no larger than the top of a barrel. Fans here had soft chair back seats and access to a great number of restrooms. Our school had hard benches to sit on and one mens' toilet down the hall from the ladies'.

Also during the warmup I watched the seats slowly begin to fill—all twelve thousand five hundred of them. Since I wasn't going to be in the starting lineup I felt less tension than those who would be in the game at the beginning.

After all the hours of practice and team meetings it was now time to get down to the business of beating the Hoosier All Star team. The horn sounded to begin the game and one minute later Mason Cooke was in control of the ball.

Halfway through the first quarter Coach Diddle noticed that our guard, Elam Webb, was having trouble keeping up with the little guy, Ron White. With three minutes left in the quarter he called in that familiar voice, "McGuire, get in there for Webb. He can't handle that little runt so you'd better do a better job of it or I'll take you out, too. Now go get him."

I checked in at the scorer's table and took a deep breath as I stepped onto the playing floor. I felt cold while the other four on our team had five minutes of sweat on their bodies. From instinct, I guess, I fell into the flow of the game keeping my eyes, feet, arms and mind alerted to the moves that Ron White might make. As reputed, he was quick but not much quicker than I was.

The game was fast with both teams running the floor when the opportunity was there. On my third trip I found myself open and took a long shot from behind the free throw circle. It went in and my confidence soared! Two trips later down the floor I hit another one, then another, and another and another all within a period of eight minutes or so. After my five goals in a row our team went ahead on the scoreboard. Man, was I wingin'!

Besides having good fortune with my shooting I was also putting the stops on Mr. White. It didn't take long for me to find that I was as quick as he was witnessed by the fact that I had held him to five points.

When the second half started I was still in the lineup in a game with the score tied. I scored three or four free throws and ended up tied as high scorer for our team. Unfortunately, we lost in the last second by three points. My biggest disappointment was in Frank Ramsey who scored only ten points and had a very average floor game. We needed a better game from him to win.

When the final horn sounded, I walked with the team back to our dressing room feeling proud that I had helped keep us in the game right up to the very end. I wished I could have hit two or three more baskets to give us a victory but it just didn't happen.

From that night of hot shooting and solid defense Mr. Diddle, who had also seen me play a good game in the state high school tournament, later offered me a scholarship including everything but my food. However, he arranged for me to eat free at a nice restaurant downtown ordering from a menu. Not bad. Better than the cafeteria food at school.

I have learned that the word "change" is a powerful word. It can make us laugh, sneeze, swear, hurt, love and do countless other things that make us happy or downright mean. Change can last for an hour, a day, a year or a lifetime.

Somehow through luck, talent or whatever, my life has run an unusual course beginning with a change in my teen years. Forever I will be grateful for what happened to me many years ago on a basketball court in Indiana.

CHAPTER THIRTY-THREE

Western Kentucky State College
September 15, 1949

Ah, college. A word that had run through my head a hundred times over the past few months. "What will it be like?" I asked myself over and over. "What do I do before class, in class, out of class?"

My brother Bobby, who had transferred from Vanderbilt to Western, was my greatest source of information. He was patient with me and my zillion questions. And living in the basketball dorm I learned even more about campus and off campus goings on.

I remember one of the early days at Western when I sat with Bobby and his friend Eddie Diddle (our coach's son) at the Goal Post, the small restaurant and hangout for nearly all students, and listened to them talk about girls they had been dating and those they were planning to ask out.

Then they talked about the spots where they could take their dates for a good time: Beach Bend amusement park with a dance pavilion, McFarland's outdoor dance floor with a jukebox and a swimming area close by, and then, of course, the Capitol theatre or the Grandview Drive Inn movie where the evening could get rather exciting.

I tried to imagine what these places looked like and wondered if I would be able to fit in with the crowds that patronized them. The mystery of it all was exciting to think about. Yeah, I was in college and I liked the feeling.

After a month or so I started getting used to my classes and the layout of the campus. There seemed to have been a hundred little walkways leading to buildings with names that meant nothing to me. One building was called Van Meter Auditorium but I was at a loss to know if it was named after some dignitary or a lovable janitor.

Basketball practice started in early October. By then I had come to know all the players I lived with and was impressed with the skills they showed in our workouts. Early on I could see that I was going to be pressed to play my best in order to stay up with the talented Western players.

I was so interested in making this college thing work that I spent a lot of time studying in the library. Most of the courses I was taking were more or less reviews of what I had taken my senior year in high school. This was a surprise.

One valuable resource we had in the Diddle home was in the lady who could make you feel at home especially in your freshman year. Louise Diddle, Mr. Diddle's wife, sewed buttons on our shirts, helped wash our laundry, tended to our colds and even let us use her kitchen for fixing our own food. She was often away playing bridge when we did this.

She was used to being around unusually big people but we shorties got the same treatment as the biggies.

With my thoughts and energy focused on playing basketball I didn't forget my girlfriend Carolyn in school at the University of Kentucky. Her frequent letters to me gave me updates of how she was doing in her first days of college.

I had seen her only twice since late September and with basketball season starting soon it would probably be several weeks before I could travel to Lexington to be with her again.

When we left home for school we agreed that both of us should date if the occasion arose. From what I heard from my all-star friend, Frank Ramsey, Carolyn was dating several different boys and had started drinking at various fraternity parties.

Carolyn didn't drink a drop when we were in high school. But at UK she had changed completely and was now partying with little thought of making good enough grades to stay in school. It's still a mystery why she changed so much so fast and set herself up to fail or nearly fail the courses she was taking.

I found time to squeeze in a trip to Lexington on a weekend when we didn't have a game. What I saw in Carolyn was a young college girl whose priorities had changed dramatically. For whatever reason she felt compelled to live the high life on campus and around town. It was sad seeing her slowly working her way toward academic failure.

I thought about Carolyn a lot. I think I loved her but then I had to wonder if I was simply fascinated with her beauty. Could it have been that? To this day I do not know.

Meanwhile, I was fighting to keep my position on the freshman team. I was in the starting lineup averaging around fourteen points a game and knew that I had to maintain that figure or close to it to stay ahead of my competition.

My skills that helped me make the first team were sharp shooting, speed and jumping ability. At five-foot-ten and one-half inches I needed all of the above to keep me ahead of the other guards.

Through the winter of 1949-1950 the varsity was having a good year and our freshman team was doing even better. By late March our season was coming to an end and for the year I was the third highest scorer on our team with an average of thirteen points a game.

Wearing a college uniform I often thought back to the time when I was too small to wear a church league jersey. I had to settle for an off color Montgomery Ward underwear shirt. That was a long time ago.

When our season ended, I made a final trip to Lexington to see if there was any way to salvage the relationship that Carolyn and I once had. She gave no hint that she wanted to break up but I felt that it was over or nearly over for us.

Two weeks after being with her I got a letter saying she thought we shouldn't see each other anymore on a regular basis. It was the perfect "Dear John" letter and I read it knowing far in advance that it would be coming sooner or later. It was over for Miss Carolyn Webb and me.

CHAPTER THIRTY-FOUR

With basketball season finished and weekends free I made it a point to get involved with the choir at the First Baptist Church. I went to choir practice on Wednesday nights and at Sunday services sang in the special numbers we had rehearsed.

I also made friends with three fellow students who had formed a barbershop quartet and were looking for someone to sing the bass voice. After a busy winter of basketball I was ready to get back into the music mode and sing some solid barbershop chords.

Jimmy Sacca, Seymour Spiegelman, Pat Maestrolio and I made up a foursome that would sing anywhere at any time. Frequently we went to the girls' dorm and sang to them through one of their open windows. They loved it and so did we. Our favorite song to croon to them was, "I'm Goin' to Sit Right Down and Write Myself a Letter". We sang that same song and others sometimes with our heads together under a campus walkway light, in the car or at a church function.

Once when we were invited to sing at the First Methodist Church the gentlemen in charge of the occasion introduced us as a group that would sing a song dedicated to "Those who are no longer with us and have gone on to heavens great shore".

Trying our best to hold our composure we walked to the front of the group and began singing two verses of "Goodbye My Coney Island Baby". The man in charge must have swallowed his tongue. We hadn't been told in advance which songs would be appropriate for the meeting so we sang what we knew how to sing.

That was the last time we performed in the downtown Methodist Church in Bowling Green.

CHAPTER THIRTY-FIVE

By the end of May we had taken our finals and were anxious to get on Highway 80 and head toward home for the summer. My first year and Bobby's third at Western were good times for both of us. We made good grades and good friends but now we were ready for some lazy days at home. Summer was coming meaning that our friends who were also in college would be home for their three months break.

Carolyn would be coming home, too. But since she sent the Dear John letter to me I was determined not to ask her out on a date. As much as I regretted our breakup, I had set my mind to stay away from her as much as I could. I was certain that this decision was not going to bring a heavy flow of tears from her.

Bobby and I, along with several friends, spent many of our summer evenings at a special venue— Don's Restaurant on Main Street. We leaned on the three parking meters in front of the store and talked about college, what might be ahead for us after we graduate and of course, girls. The last subject always seemed to get more attention than the other two.

The summer of 1950 seemed to fly by. Before we knew it the time had come for us to pack our bags and head back to Western for the fall semester registration. Mother had spoiled us with her tolerance for our sleeping till noon and eating breakfast at one o'clock in the afternoon. However, all that was about to end. Ahead was the return to eight o'clock classes, late night studying and volunteer workouts at the gym.

With Carolyn no longer a major figure in my life I began dating some of the young ladies I had met in class or at other places around the campus.

I also returned to the First Baptist Church choir for rehearsals and singing at the Sunday morning services. Music was still very important to me. Besides singing in the church choir I was now a member of two barbershop quartets that sang around town and on campus.

Both groups sang good harmony but the one with Jimmy Sacca, Seymour Spiegelman, Pat Maestrolio and me sang in a higher range giving the chords a more distinct ring.

Then came October once again and basketball practices. I had been put on full scholarship losing my downtown restaurant privileges to the school cafeteria with its mysterious casseroles and fried-to-death pork chops.

When practices started I found what I already knew to be true: the quality of my competition had increased considerably over the freshman team I had played on. Senior

Showing off my first letter earned in college

guards with three years playing experience were tough to handle and even tougher to score on. Playing time for me during the 1950-1951 season was going to be hard to come by.

1950-51 Basketball team – Western Kentucky State College
Second row L-R Coach Diddle, me, brother Bobby

Bobby was in the same position. When he played at Vanderbilt he was always at the forward position. In high school he played the center or pivot slot. Never had he played in a game where he faced the man guarding him.

Also, he had taken few shots from the guard position. Facing the basket while trying to shoot the ball was not comfortable for him.

When the season started, Bobby and I were warming the bench. The only time we were in a game together was against Evansville College where I managed to score five points and him none. Playing time was limited for both of us and by the middle of the season we were fortunate to get any time at all on the court.

But just being on the traveling squad was quite an honor. I had my first plane ride on a DC 3 to New York, Philadelphia and Buffalo where we played LIU, LaSalle, and Saint Bonaventure all in one week.

The LIU game was played in Madison Square Garden, which was a thrill for all of us. When told that we would be using former heavyweight champion Joe Louis' dressing room I was impressed. After all, he had been one of the biggest sports figures in America so I had reason to feel honored to be dressing on hallowed ground.

Bobby and I were a long way from Hazard and we loved every minute of our trip to the big cities. When we got back to Bowling Green I told some friends about climbing to the top row of Madison Square Garden and looking over the arena where so many important sporting events had been held. The Garden seated nearly eighteen thousand people, which at the time was an unheard of figure for indoor sporting events.

The season ended with us playing in what was called, "The All Campus Tournament" at Bradley University. The point shaving scandal had been uncovered in New York and "Back To The Campus" tournaments sprang up all over the country.

Against Bradley I played about five minutes, proudly scoring two baskets on All American, Gene Melchoire. We lost the game by five points, headed back to Bowling Green and hung up our uniforms for another year.

Bobby graduated in June then enrolled at UK to begin work on his master's degree. Instead of going home for the summer I decided to go to summer school and take classes that would help lighten my schedule somewhat for the fall semester. Five other players and I had free rein in the dorm and Mr. Diddle, a fanatic about keeping his house in order, helped me paint my room.

He and I made a critical mistake in choosing the proper paint to cover the walls. We thought all paint was pretty much the same but soon found that enamel was not meant to be applied to ceilings or walls.

After we finished our two hours of painting and the paint dried overnight, we discovered that we could comb our hair and shave looking into the wall as shiny as a mirror. Neither of us said a word to each other about the ignorance we showed in choosing the wrong paint.

When summer school was out I went home for only two weeks before returning to campus. It was a short summer in Hazard but at least I had a few days to relax before starting my third year at Western.

CHAPTER THIRTY-SIX

While I was going through the frustrating days of being an inactive player I found one bright spot not at all related to basketball.

After practice one day Charlie Rawlings and I were waiting in line in the cafeteria when I spotted a pretty young girl I hadn't seen on campus all year. She was with my friend Margaret Ross and quickly I began making plans to meet the newly discovered girl through Margaret's introduction.

Hurriedly, I finished my supper from the cafeteria metal tray and made my way to where Margaret and her friend were sitting. I spoke to my friend and nodded a hello to her companion. Margaret, seeing my face all lit up knew that I was jockeying for an introduction to the young lady sitting next to her. She didn't disappoint me saying, "Don, I'd like you to meet Maxine McIntosh who, like me, is from Owensboro. She's a freshman this year. And Maxine, this is Don McGuire, a junior here on the hill and a member of the basketball team."

Maxine and I smiled hello at each other with me already hoping this wouldn't be the last time we'd see each other.

Man o' man, was Maxine pretty! She had a wide smile that showed beautiful teeth and lit up the flawless skin on her face. She was just about the best looking girl I'd ever seen. After our brief conversation I went back to the table where Charlie was still sitting waiting for me. He had seen what I'd been doing over the past few minutes and, common to his nature, had something cute to say about my visit with the two girls.

"Fall in love did ya'? I mean the way you looked at that pretty thing I knew you were fallin' fast."

"Haven't fallen yet, Charlie. But I swear I think that young lady is the best looking girl I've ever seen."

"Whoa now boy. That's sayin' an awful lot. Surely you've seen other girls on this campus as pretty as, uh, what's her name?"

"Maxine. Maxine McIntosh."

"Yeah, Maxine. Well anyway, if you think she's that good lookin' I guess I can't argue with you."

"No need to. And you know what Charlie, someday I'd like to marry a girl that looks like Maxine. Right now I don't know much about her but you can bet your last dime that I'm goin' to change all that. Margaret will help me."

CHAPTER THIRTY-SEVEN

In the 1951-1952 season my position on the basketball team was going to be tenuous to say the least. The year before Mr. Diddle had recruited five super talented freshman from Tennessee and Indiana and suddenly I found myself moving farther and farther down the bench when the season started.

The 1951-1952 team was led by an extremely gifted player named Tom Marshall from Mt. Juliet, Tennessee. He and the other outstanding players comprised a team that would be highly ranked in the national polls.

Regardless of the overload of talent on that year's team, I kept plugging along trying to get in some playing time. I managed to get in the Cincinnati game for five minutes or so but didn't score any points.

Nearing the end of the season I realized that my basketball career was slowly heading for retirement. Regardless of this admission I kept practicing hard every day hoping that a chance to play more would come my way. It didn't.

The 1952 season ended with Western having a 24-5 season, including two wins in the National Invitational Tournament. I took off my uniform for the last time and admitted with regret that my playing days were over.

But all was not over as far as Mr. Diddle was concerned. He had heard from someone that I had been a pretty good pitcher in high school and on the American Legion team in Hazard. He told me that he was one pitcher short on his roster and wanted me to fill that spot for him.

So, to start the season on a very cool April afternoon there I stood on the mound waiting for the first batter from a college in Illinois to come to the plate. Despite the very uncomfortable weather, I managed to go the full game allowing only three hits and winning 7-1. Surprise! My days as an athlete weren't over after all.

College baseball schedules in the fifties weren't very long. We played only a dozen or so against teams in the Ohio Valley Conference, at Fort Knox (where I pitched and won again) and in the conference tournament.

I was the starting pitcher in the Ohio Valley Conference championship game against Hazardite Don Feltner of Eastern Kentucky State College. I went four innings before being relieved with us ahead 5-2. We won the championship when six-foot-ten-inch Art Spoelstra completely shut out Eastern after I left the game.

Once again I peeled off this-is-my-last-game jersey and spent time getting to know Maxine as the semester rolled on.

CHAPTER THIRTY-EIGHT

April 1952

I was caught off guard in a pleasant way when the lead singer in our barbershop quartet asked me a question as we sat together in a booth at the Goal Post Restaurant. Jimmy Sacca asked if I would be interested in making a demonstration tape of two tunes his friend had written. With a phony look of confidence, I answered, "Yeah, I'm interested. I haven't made a demo this week."

Hellfire, I didn't know what a demonstration tape was! But I soon learned when I met the shy little fellow who wrote the songs we were to record.

Billy Vaughn, our composer, played piano at the Boots and Saddle Club in Bowling Green for seventy-five dollars a week. He paid forty dollars a month for rent, had no car, no washing machine and of course no extra money. We soon found out that he was loaded with music talent.

Billy, age 32, could play nine instruments, write a good love song in an hour and make musical arrangements for any orchestra in the country. Problem was he'd never had an outlet for all the talent in his genius brain. But the time to begin uncovering his music skills was about to begin.

Jimmy also asked Seymour Spiegelman and Russ Brown to help tape record Billy's songs but Russ said he didn't have time to rehearse and record with us. This being only a rough copy of the songs to be recorded, Billy said, "Oh, I'll just go ahead and sing Russ' part. It's only a demo."

So, on April 10, 1952 the first sound of Billy Vaughn's tune called

"Trying" came off a rough but adequate $30.00 tape recorder in Van Meter Auditorium on Western's campus. For such an inexpensive recorder the sound wasn't too bad.

Following at least twenty recordings of "Trying" we finally made the one that sounded better than all the previous takes. The second song "You Made Up My Mind" was done in about a dozen tries. And in two hours or so Billy's tunes were on tape for the first time ready to be played somewhere on the air.

"Somewhere" meant radio station WLBJ in Bowling Green. Bill Stamps, a popular disc jockey at that station was very receptive to our request to play "Trying" on his evening pop music show. So, in the early hours of his show the large audience that listened to Stamps every night heard the song for the first time.

The reception to the first airing of "Trying" was gratifying. The students at Western knew who had recorded the song and kept calling in over and over asking Stamps to play it again. There must have been at least ten calls in a one hour period making the requests.

Jimmy, Seymour, Billy and I were pleasantly shocked to hear so many people asking to hear the simple tune that Billy wrote. Now the question was what do we do with the tape? Where do we send it and to whom?

Enter Bill Stamps again. It happened that Bill had worked for Randy Wood, the creator and operator of a small record company called Dot records. The home office was in Gallatin, Tennessee about twenty-four miles from Nashville. The company had never had a hit but consistently sold enough records to stay in business.

Convinced that Randy Wood would give the tape a good listening, Bill sent it to the Dot office asking for an opinion regarding the songs and the singers. The hope was that Randy would like both and agree to record the group.

In the middle of April Randy received the tape in the mail and curiously listened to it more than once. He played it for the employees in his record shop and even for the two ladies who cleaned his home each week. He also played it for anyone around who would take the time to listen and give an opinion.

Finally after one week of what-do-you-thinks he decided to get in touch with Bill Stamps and tell him that Dot was interested in recording the tunes on the tape. Excitedly, Stamps immediately called Billy to give him the good news. And of course, Billy contacted Jimmy, Seymour, and me to tell us that we were going to be on Dot records.

CHAPTER THIRTY-NINE

Randy Wood, President of Dot Records, was born an entrepreneur. When he was in college he operated a food cart in his dormitory every night of the week. Long after the dinner hour he would push his cart up and down the halls selling Cokes, sandwiches, cigarettes and candy. What he earned in his business helped pay his tuition and other fees the college charged.

Randy served in World II and after being discharged settled in Gallatin, Tennessee. He quickly became a part of the town's economy by opening a small appliance repair shop. Even though he was making a decent living fixing toasters and such he fulfilled one of his ambitions by becoming the owner of a phonograph record shop.

At first business was slow. But Randy, always the positive one, felt that in time his establishment would be a profitable endeavor. And it was.

A fully stocked record store carrying many different artists' works soon began drawing customers from as far away as Nashville.

With his shop now showing a handsome profit, his business astuteness once again came into play. Instead of operating only a record store he began expanding his business considerably by making it a mail order record shop. With good promotion that operation could help sell records all around the Midwest and the South.

One year after the new business was in place Randy created a motto for his operation and called it "The largest mail order record shop in the world". True or not, it was remarkable that he could build a thriving enterprise in such a short span of time.

Next, Randy made a questionable move when he decided to go into the recording business. He had no experience dealing with such a volatile industry and questioned himself about his decision to enter a highly competitive business. Admitting his limited knowledge of the complex inner workings of record producing, he nevertheless decided to stay the course and compete with the major labels.

Despite his doubts, Randy gave birth to Dot Records in 1949. His first two signees were Johnny Maddox, a ragtime piano player and country singer, Mack Wiseman. Record sales were modest for both artists but the income they generated was enough to help keep the Dot label alive.

Randy's hope to get a foothold in the record business might possibly come to fruition if the songs on a demonstration tape of a vocal group from Bowling Green, Kentucky could prove to have hit quality. Odds were against him that this unknown quartet could give the company a kick start. But he was determined to give all his energy and most of Dot Record's bank account to try to beat the odds.

CHAPTER FORTY

Even before we thought about making a record I knew the four voices that would be on the recording were all different. Lead singer Jimmy, tenor, Seymour, baritone, Billy and I, the bass, had an unusually good blend, giving the harmony a simple but commercial sound.

Jimmy was a strong lead singer. His voice was blessed with fine timbre and quality that gave him a distinct sound. He would be the main voice of The Hilltoppers with the three of us supplying background harmony.

In college Jimmy would sing anywhere there was a crowd and a piano. When big bands came to Bowling Green for concerts or dances, his best friend, Bill Ploumis, would front for him. Bill, six-feet-three-inches tall and as strong as a young bull would catch the bandleader during a break and say to me, "Look mister bandman, I gotta' buddy that sings and he's gonna' sing the next number. If you have any questions you come to me. Understand?" Rarely did Jimmy miss a guest shot with a band that came to Bowling Green.

Seymour had a solo voice with outstanding range. When asked at any party to sing his favorite song the tune would always be, "Our Love Is Here To Stay". He was active in Western's music department, often singing in the college choir or in a mixed quartet. He would be the perfect tenor in any vocal group.

Billy was a musician with perfect pitch. In our practice for a session he would always let us know immediately if one or more of us happened to be out of tune. His singing voice was not of solo quality, but when harmonizing he was always on key. He was the absolute master at directing the band, playing the piano and singing his part all at the same time.

Then there was me. Usually I stuck a finger into my ear to hear myself and try to stay in tune. I didn't have perfect pitch so I simply had to stay on my toes and think "in tune" when singing with a group. I was never a soloist. This was due to my lack of range and voice quality.

In a barbershop quartet I could sing either the tenor, baritone or bass parts with good intonation. I always had a way of blending with other voices to make solid harmony.

And so ends the review of the voices that were about to be recorded on Dot Records in Van Meter Auditorium at Western Kentucky State College. Wonder what's going to happen?

CHAPTER FORTY-ONE

The session was set for April 20 at the venue where the original taping took place. Randy liked the echo sound he heard on the tape and decided to get the same effect on his professional recording equipment.

And so the big night came. Getting into Van Meter after working hours was not easy. Randy had to pay the campus policeman ten dollars to open the doors to use for about four hours. Aubrey Homan, Western's only law enforcer, reluctantly let us use the auditorium but only till elven o'clock.

While setting up the portable recording equipment a few friends plus Maxine, Jeannie (Seymour's fiancé), Ann (Jimmy's fiancé) and Billy's wife, Smitty were all that were present to watch and listen to the recording session. To this day at least one thousand people have claimed being at our first session.

When Randy was set to start, he and his assistant, Al Bennett, were notified by Billy that the soft pedal on the grand piano would not stay in the down position. To remedy the problem Jimmy's friend, Bill Ploumis volunteered to lie on the floor and hold down the defective pedal when each take was in progress.

Bill was on the football team at Western so having enough strength to do the job was no problem. The only uncomfortable part of it all was Bill having to get up and down from the floor for four hours.

When all was set to make the first cut I knew that the four of us were feeling a touch of tension knowing our debut as recording artists was about to begin. The setup for the session was as bare-boned as we would ever see again. A piano, four voices, a tape recorder, two technicians and a pedal holder were set to do something that might have a chance of making all of us a part of music history.

When the recording session began all nervousness was forgotten. The effort to stay in tune and make a good recording was our first priority. And we kept it that way through the initial takes on the recorder.

"Let's do it one more time," was still being the call from Randy or Al even after what we thought were good takes. The last four bars of "Trying" were a bit tricky but we managed to handle the problem with ease.

"Trying. Take Fifteen. Dot Records 486504." That call was recorded first to identify what was coming on the next recording. We were now at number twenty and even though we thought most of the takes were good, Randy was not sold on any of them.

Finally, after about the thirtieth recording which we thought had the weakest ending of all the previous ones, Randy gave us a thumbs-up and said, "That one's it. That's the keeper."

"That's what?" Jimmy asked. "It can't be. That's the weakest ending we've done so far."

"It's not that weak. That's the first one we've done that had the feel.

"Randy, are you saying that 'the feel' as you call it wasn't in any of the other takes?"

"No, it wasn't. It took all this time to get the one that I've been waiting for. Now we have it."

The four of us were disappointed that Randy didn't use one of the other takes with a perfect ending. But he didn't and we had no choice but to accept his decision on the matter.

Recording Billy's "You Made Up My Mind" took far less time than did "Trying". It was a cute up tempo tune that was to be the "B" or backside on the records. Finally around 10:30 the session was over and Randy gathered his equipment and our songs and said, "Goodbye, thanks, and I'll talk to you soon," then headed back toward Gallatin.

The friends and fiances' watching the session had grown a bit weary from the four long hours of sitting and staying quiet. Jimmy, Seymour, and I took our girlfriends out for a late snack and reviewed the session just finished. All agreed that what we did that night was indeed an unusual happening for three college boys and a struggling piano player. Now we would have to be patient waiting to hear when the first records would be pressed and sent to disc jockeys for review and air time.

CHAPTER FORTY-TWO

Two weeks after the recording session Randy called to tell us that "Trying" was now in the hands of all the major disc jockeys in the South and Midwest. He had also set up distributorships in major cities around the country. They were the ones who made sure that record shops had sufficient supplies of hits and non-hits to sell to the public.

Preliminary reports from the major cities gave no indication that "Trying" was making any noise in the market. But it was still early and Randy was making a tour of some of the Midwest cities to promote the record at radio and TV stations.

By the middle of May, four weeks after our recording session, we were still not hearing any good news at all from Randy. The record was being played but nobody was buying. It appeared that the public wasn't interested in Billy's song. If they were surely there would have already been some sales somewhere.

After the fifth and sixth weeks passed, Randy felt certain that "Trying" wasn't going to make it in the market. Convinced of this, he called and asked that we come to Gallatin to talk about another recording session with new songs. Heeding Randy's call, we drove to Gallatin on a Friday afternoon with our feathers down from disappointment.

As we sat in his office we began discussing what type of song we should record in the next session. Suggestions were offered ranging from up-tempo tunes to country and western. While trying to decide which direction we should go, the phone rang and Randy excused himself from our discussion to answer the call.

He was quiet for a few seconds listening to whomever it was on the other end. Five minutes after the phone rang Randy hung up after saying only a few words to the party that had called. He then turned to look at us with a super wide smile and said, "That was Izzy Nathan on the phone from Cincinnati. In a very excited voice Izzy said, 'I don't know who this group is that did the song "Trying" and I don't give a damn. As fast as you can get one thousand records to me. This thing is hot up here and I gotta' get it into the record shops real fast."

The four of us were stunned even more when the phone rang again an hour later with the Cleveland distributor on the line. His excitement equaled the Cincinnati distributor's as he said, "Hey Randy, you've got somethin' goin' up here with this record "Trying". Get your rear end in gear and send two thousand records to my warehouse so I can scatter them around town to the stores."

Unbelievable.

The five of us sat there and watched and heard a record break into popularity in the Midwest. Randy was smiling. All of us were smiling. We really didn't know what to say about what seemed to be a miracle.

The following week St. Louis, Pittsburgh and New York called ordering copies of "Trying". The song had begun to hit in those towns too and Randy was shipping records as fast as they could be pressed.

After all those days of sweating out the destiny of Billy's tune we now knew that we had a hit on our hands. Now what? One of the first things we had to do was to get a name for ourselves. The Four Dingos? The Four Tunes? What? We should have known that Randy already had a name picked out for us. As clever as he was there was no doubt that he would choose a name with some meaning to it.

Were we students at Western Kentucky State College? Don't our daily lives revolve around the school? Isn't the nickname of the college athletic teams the "Hilltoppers"?

To Randy it was a no brainer. We were Hilltopper students yesterday. The next day we became Hilltopper singers. Issue settled.

CHAPTER FORTY-THREE

July 10, 1952—Billboard Magazine—"Trying" by the Hilltoppers #20
Cashbox Magazine—"Trying" by the Hilltoppers #15

The two most important magazines in the music industry were ranking our song higher each week. In the beginning the song was listed at #100 then #50, #30, #25, #20. And finally in early fall, "Trying" jumped into the number five slot ahead of most of the major artists in the music business.

And where were we when the ranking magazines put us in the top five songs in America?

Dazed.

But Randy wouldn't let us stay that way. He scheduled us on the live morning show at Nashville's WSM radio with a full orchestra playing behind us. We worked there with the Anita Kerr Singers and Chet Adkins on our first ever 50,000 watt radio appearance.

Next was a local TV show with a studio about as large as the inside of a car. After that minor production we visited virtually every disc jockey in Nashville promoting our song. Nashville was "Trying's" hottest town in the country and we worked hard to keep it that way.

But through all the early days of our controlled mania there still loomed things called school, classes, tests, things that we had to attend to in order to keep our draft boards from taking us into the Armed Services. Leaving school would automatically make us eligible for induction.

With our song riding high, personal appearance requests began coming into the offices of our new booking agency MCA. Although in demand, we were not ready to try to entertain audiences. We had not a hint of stage training.

Without our knowing it, Randy was working hard to get us on national television in New York. Of course MCA was a powerful agency using their clout to help him find national exposure for us.

After days of hustling the major networks for TV time, MCA hit the jackpot. An agreement was drawn up for us to appear on what was considered to be the most powerful TV show in America. In two weeks we were to appear on the Ed Sullivan show at the CBS studio in New York.

"WOW!" Now we were topping off all the promoting we had been doing by appearing on the daddy of all TV shows. Mr. Sullivan was known as the most powerful figure in network television. He had the clout to make or break people in the entertainment business.

With the show only days away there were some quick decisions that needed to be made. The three major ones were: how do we get to New York? What are we going to wear during the three or four minutes that we will be on the air? Where do we stay for three days while in the city?

As usual, Randy had already made plans for what we thought to be major issues. Since we had very little money between us he offered to buy airplane tickets with no charge to us. We refused his generous offer. We felt that four tickets would be very expensive for him and the cost of the trip should not be his responsibility to bankroll. However, Dot Records was going to be pick up food and hotel costs.

So how do we get to the big city? Answer: in Jimmy's dad's car which he had driven from his home in Lockport, New York to Bowling Green the previous month.

What will we wear on the show? Mr. Sullivan and Randy, with his creativity, suggested wearing letter sweaters with W's on the front. That didn't sound so bad. But when the next suggestion was for us to wear sissy looking beanies, I thought I would throw up. Beanies on national television? Why not new tuxedos? Sport clothes? Even long johns. Anything but those dadgum beanies.

I lost the argument. Sweaters it would be. Beanies too.

CHAPTER FORTY-FOUR

The trip to New York took twelve hours. We drove all night, each of us taking turns driving a shift of about two hours. Finally arriving in Manhattan, we made our way through a very crowded Times Square and with some difficulty finally found the Warwick Hotel.

Randy was already there along with Bobby Brenner, the MCA agent we would be working with during our stay. After introductions the six of us sat down and began going over plans that we would be following up to and after the Sullivan show.

"Tomorrow we have an appointment with Jon Gregory. He's the best choreographer in the city who will get you ready for your TV appearance," Bobby informed us.

A choreographer? I didn't know if Jon Gregory was going to fix my teeth or work on my shoes. We didn't have one of those in Hazard. I was later informed that this person taught performers how to move their hands, feet and bodies to make them look graceful and professional while performing.

According to Bobby, Jon had worked with the best actors and singing groups in the entertainment business. He had just finished choreographing a movie in Hollywood called, "She's Working Her Way Through College" staring Virginia Mayo. Apparently he would be teaching us how and when to move while singing our song in front of cameras.

The following morning we were in Nola Studios learning how to sway back and forth in unison and change places at the bridge or middle of the tune.

Nola's was a rehearsal studio. Down the hall from us we could hear Perry Como and Eddie Fisher practicing for their network shows. Other artists were rehearsing their acts for stage shows and television appearances. I was impressed.

The day of the Sullivan show we took a cab to the CBS studios where we would rehearse our spot on the program. It was shortly after one thirty when we walked through the gigantic doors of the building into a studio buzzing with activity.

June Christy was on stage rehearsing her song for the show.

Sitting in the front row of the audience seats was Henry Fonda who was to be interviewed on the air by Mr. Sullivan. Seeing all that was going on around us we realized that we were a long way from the Goal Post and Van Meter Auditorium at Western. This was the big time, the top rung of the show business ladder. We were standing in the studio of the most popular show in the United States. What a feeling!

While waiting our turn to rehearse, a gentleman with a camera around his neck stopped by and asked if we would mind if he interviewed us. Of course we told him we would be delighted to answer his questions after he told us who he worked for.

"I'm from Newsweek," he explained. "I work in the entertainment section of the magazine and do interviews with the guests on Mr. Sullivan's show each week."

"Did you say Newsweek? Newsweek Magazine?" Seymour skeptically asked our visitor.

"Yes. I'm with Newsweek."

"Why do you want to interview us? After all we're not the most powerful act in the business." Seymour continued.

"Maybe not," he returned. "But you're a gimmick."

"What do you mean by a gimmick? How'd we get that tag?" I asked.

"It means that you are four college kids with a hit record on the biggest show in the country. That's interesting news and a show business gimmick," he answered.

"Well then, have a go at it. We're ready to answer any questions you might want to ask," Seymour approved. "Even though we are a gimmick."

Around two o'clock it came our turn to rehearse "Trying" on stage. After taking our designated position the band gave us a solid introduction and we began singing. From then on the piano took over giving out the same sound that's on the record.

Rehearsing for the Ed Sullivan Show; nerves beginning to fire up

Unfortunately, we weren't able to hear the piano since it was so far away from us. Because of this arrangement we got out of tune and were grossly embarrassed in front of the entire studio crew. This was not good.

Jimmy apologized for our musical blunder and asked that the piano be moved closer to the stage where we could hear it clearer and stay on key. A crew of six men lifted the piano up on the stage to no more than ten feet from our assigned spot. After that there were no more bad notes hit during rehearsal.

CHAPTER FORTY-FIVE

After rehearsal we went to our dressing room to relax an hour or so before the show. As we were settling in, one of the young stagehands stuck his head in the door and said, "It's makeup time for the four of you so come with me to get your faces worked on."

Makeup time? I hadn't even thought about makeup. But now we were about to be escorted somewhere to have special things done to us I surmised.

Our escort took us to a brightly lit room with six barbershop style chairs lined in a row. This was new territory to us.

"Sir," a pretty young lady hailed me with a smile. "You may come to my chair so that I can do my job and beautify you for the show. You other three can take seats in the remaining chairs. Someone will be with you shortly."

Heading her call, I stepped onto the footrest and then sat on the cushioned seat. Joking, I said, "You're not going to hurt me are you? Promise me you won't."

"You can relax. I'm not going to hurt you one bit. I'm simply going to make you more handsome than you've ever been. And I guarantee you that you won't know yourself when I finish working on that face."

Next, the back of the chair was put into a slight reclining position, a towel was spread over my upper chest and the young lady began applying makeup.

Ah, what a wonderful feeling it was to be pampered by the hands of a trained specialist. "Eat your hearts out peons of Hazard and Big Bottom! Your old buddy is now in the luxurious lap of the gods!"

The entire procedure took about twenty minutes to complete. When the artist had finished with me she raised my chair back to the upright position and said, "Now take a look at yourself in the mirror straight ahead of you."

I did what she suggested and at the first sight of my pampered face I asked, "Who's that? I don't think I know that gentleman."

"It's you and nobody else," the lady confirmed. "You're now ready to have the CBS camera focus on you. Good luck out there."

I thanked her then looked at Seymour, Jimmy and Billy and snickered at their made up faces. With a deep tan on all of us we appeared to have been lying in the tanning bed for a long spell. The unfamiliar procedure performed by skilled hands was a first for all of us.

CHAPTER FORTY-SIX

It took only a short time for citizens of Hazard to pass the word that one of their boys was going to be on network television's most popular show, the Ed Sullivan show. Many of them, including my parents of course, had been planning to watch the show together at a neighbor's house. It was a first for this small town to have a former resident appearing on such a powerful show.

Of course Asher and Pearl McGuire were in another world knowing that their youngest boy had hit the big time. With a tear jerking song called "Trying" The Hilltoppers' first recording was currently ranked number five in the nation.

Asher, who had a tendency to brag on The Hilltoppers, declared, "My boy is goin' to be on television this Sunday night. He and his buddies are in New York right now practicing to be on the biggest TV show in America. Now that's rare to have one of us here in Hazard to be makin' it big time in the big city. Yep, my boy's right there."

On rare occasions when I could visit Mother and Daddy in Hazard I soon found that my name had been changed from Don to "my boy". Friends kidded me about my new moniker. But they understood that Asher McGuire's extra pride in his son's accomplishments was justified.

On the air with Ed Sullivan – 40 million people watching

Mother Pearl was not one to shout to the world The Hilltoppers' success story. She was proud of our good fortune but unlike her husband kept her feelings regarding our success to herself. When someone would ask her how she felt having a celebrity son she would invariably reply, "He's a good boy. I'm proud that he and the others have had the chance to go as far as they have. It's a wonderful story and I'm very happy to be the mother of one of The Hilltoppers. My boy's dad was happy about it, too."

Mother and Daddy saw us perform only once. That was in Indianapolis where I had a nerve attack because they were in the audience. It seemed that I always got a bit shaky when someone I knew was at our show. Why? I really don't know. Maybe it was because I wanted us to look and sound our best performing in front of a friend or relative. We always did.

CHAPTER FORTY-SEVEN

Showtime!!!Blinding stage lights. Jumpy nerves. Fake smiles and talented show people anxiously waiting to do their thing on a celebrated stage. Three different acts including Henry Fonda went on before the time came to do our thing. Two minutes before our appearances the stage manager came up to me and asked, "How are you going to feel in two minutes with forty million people looking at you?"

I nearly peed.

But fortunately I didn't and after a brief interview with Mr. Sullivan we did our three minute song without a hitch. Generous applause brought us back for a second bow.

After we trotted off stage into the wing one of my friends from Hazard who happened to be in New York said to Seymour, "You guys sounded great but Seymour, why didn't you smile?"

Seymour looked directly into my friend's eyes and said, "If I had smiled I would have vomited." So much said for the pressure that was on us to do our best.

With the Sullivan show behind us we knew that we had to have help getting us to look good on stage. The singing was in good order but looking like professionals was something we would have to work on. Return to Jon Gregory.

Fifteen songs. That's what we would need to go on club stages and entertain people who had paid to see and hear us. Hiring Jon to stage these tunes was a must. There was no way we could do it by ourselves. So, get out the pocketbook. His cost, paid by Randy and Dot records, was fifteen hundred dollars, a fortune to us at the time.

In order to stage our act we were to miss three days of classes. This wasn't good. Fortunately, our professors were more than cooperative in allowing us to stay in New York without giving unexcused absences.

On the third day of our training, Jon suggested that we go across the street to the Paramount theatre to see the Four Aces, the number one vocal group in the country. He had staged their act two years earlier and wanted us to see how they used his training in front of a thousand or more people.

Once in the theatre we went upstairs to the Four Aces dressing room shortly before their part of the show was to begin. Each of the four greeted Jon with hearty handshakes and introduced themselves to us. What a great feeling it was to meet the guys we had listened to on jukeboxes and radios at school. They were famous in the music business and favorites of the teenagers who were buying their records like crazy.

A few minutes after we came into their dressing room a loud voice from the bottom of the steps called to the Aces saying, "YA' GOT TEN MINUTES BEFORE SHOW!. TEN MINUTES!.."

That meant the quartet would shortly be going in front of a full house to sing their hits. This thought concerned me. We had never sung before that many people or even half that many.

After leaving the Four Aces' dressing room we bought tickets for five and found our seats halfway down the aisle. At the time the theatre was nearly dark and the moment for the stars to appear was only a few seconds away.

Then without expecting it, a drum roll came from the rear of the orchestra and an authoritative voice began the introduction of the Aces—
"AND NOW, LADIES AND GENTLEMEN, THE PARAMOUNT THEATRE PROUDLY PRESENTS THE NUMBER ONE SINGING GROUP IN AMERICA, A GROUP WE KNOW YOU'RE GOING TO ENJOY! LET'S GIVE A BIG NEW YORK WELCOME TO— THE FOUR ACES!"

The second he said Aces two of them came from the left side of the stage, the other two from the right side and met at the microphone that had just risen from floor level. At the mic the four hit their opening song in perfect rhythm with the band — "SHOULD I REVEAL EXACTLY HOW I FEEL, SHOULD I TELL YOU BABY THAT I LOVE YOU".

Around us the kids were going crazy at the sound that had become so popular. The band is blowing the hinges off the doors, the lights are flashing and the Aces are doing Jon Gregory's moves on stage. It was wild.

Watching the group putting on their stage smiles, hearing them singing their parts and working in front of so many people I suddenly felt a hint of doubt regarding our future stage appearances.

Halfway through the opening number I turned to Jon sitting next to me and said, "Jon, I don't know if I can do what they're doing up there. They're remembering their moves, their vocal parts and they're smiling at the crowd. I just don't know if I can handle all that."

Jon turned toward me and said above the crowd noise, "Don, believe me, you're going to do it and I promise that you will. Stay positive. I'm going to get you ready for the biggest stages in this country. That you can bank on."

Believing in Jon's assurance that I and the other three would be ready to perform with confidence, we left New York and flew back to Bowling Green. His teaching of movement on the stage would undoubtedly make us look professional if we executed what he had taught us.

CHAPTER FORTY-EIGHT

The weeks following the hours we spent with Jon found us trying to find time to go to classes and work on weekends at night spots all around the Midwest. Akron, Cleveland, Chicago, Indianapolis and other cities had clubs asking for our appearance from Friday nights till late Sunday evening. To get to these towns and then back to school by Monday morning meant chartering an airplane to move us around the country. Many times I would come into an eight o'clock class with a trace of makeup still on my face. It was five days of going to school and three nights and days of entertaining somewhere where we were running hot.

While "Trying" was still holding its own we released two recordings that didn't make it on the charts. Finally, in order to follow up on our first successful recording we went to Nashville in hopes of finding a tune that would fit our style. We needed to score another best seller to hold our position in the popularity polls.

Billy had written a tear jerking country and western song called "I'd Rather Die Young" which had hit potential backed with Randy's favorite college tune, "P.S. I Love You". Billy's song was considered the "A" side while "P.S." was recorded simply to put something on the flip side.

With the word die in the title we learned that disc jockeys in many northern towns refused to play the record on their shows. Consequently, the same DJ's flipped to the other side of the recording and played "P.S." until it began gaining popularity.

Meanwhile in the south, DJ's loved Billy's new song with the word die having absolutely no negative feedback. They played it over and over and gave "P.S." some air time, too.

After the record had been out a month or so we found that "P.S." was moving up fast on the charts only a few weeks after being released and it took over the lead from Billy's tune. The unexpected hit jumped to the number twenty spot in Billboard Magazine.

Suddenly we had a two-sided hit going and the orders were beginning to pour in. At one time Randy told us that he was shipping 30,000 records a day of "I'd Rather Die Young" and "P.S. I Love You" to all parts of the country. Now instead of being a one hit quartet we were backing "Trying's" success with what appeared to be a much bigger seller.

In early December of 1952, "P.S." made a dramatic leap to the number ten slot in the trade magazines. By late December it moved even further up the list of top songs finally settling in at number three.

When 1953 made it's debut, "Trying" was still a strong seller and "P.S." was burning up the charts. With both tunes hot on the record market, requests for us to do personal appearances around the country more than doubled. The Hilltoppers were now prepared to face the large audiences. Jon Gregory's choreography and a few months experience were gradually making us into an act worth paying to see.

At Western Kentucky State: left to right – Kelly Thompson,
Assistant to the President; Jimmy, Seymour, Me, and Billy.

CHAPTER FORTY-NINE

MCA, with its power and push, landed us a first-class booking. With a reputation for featuring only the biggest stars, the Chicago Theatre was our next stop. It was a huge showplace with what seemed to be a million blinking lights under the marque. And in tall letters above the lights was— **"STARTING TODAY—THE HILLTOPPERS"**. What a great feeling it was to see our name up there where so many top stars had also been featured!

Once we arrived for the first show we settled into our rather plush dressing room and began putting on our New York City tailor-made tuxedos. Then with the usual hint of tenseness we made our way to the wings and listened to the announcement that would put us in front of a packed house.

"AND NOW, LADIES AND GENTLEMEN FOR YOUR ENTERTAINMENT AND PLEASURE THE CHICAGO THEATRE PROUDLY PRESENTS AMERICA'S NUMBER ONE VOCAL GROUP WITH JIMMY SACCA, BILLY VAUGHN, SEYMOUR SPIEGELMAN AND DON MCGUIRE. LET'S WELCOME THE STARS OF OUR SHOW—THE HILLTOPPERS!!"

At the sound of our name Billy and I came from the left side of the stage and Jimmy and Seymour entered from the right side ala the Four Aces. The microphone came up from the floor and we did it. We did Jon Gregory's moves, sang our parts and smiled as the young audience of approximately twelve hundred responded to our entrance and performance.

One afternoon between shows our local record company agent took us for an interview with Chicago's most powerful TV personality, Irv Cupsinet. Once at the studio we were told that other guests were being interviewed and that we would have to wait our turn to be on the show.

When Mr. Cupsinet learned that we were waiting outside the studio door he came and invited us to come in and meet the guests who were already there. It so happened that he had been interviewing actors Charlton Heston, Paul Douglas and his wife Jan Sterling.

We met them, found the three to be very friendly and invited them to come to one of our shows. Later we learned that they were in the audience at our 4:00 P.M. appearance. We considered it an honor to have three well known movie stars taking time to watch us perform.

Doing thirty-six shows in six days during Christmas did a number of positive things for us. One, it gave us the opportunity to refine our act and number two, it taught us to appreciate fans who gave time and money to watch us perform.

One of the tougher parts of the engagement was signing autographs for the crowds that always gathered after each show just outside the stage door.

Following each performance we had two hours or so to go back to the hotel for a quick rest, to eat lunch or just relax for a few minutes. But once we finished signing autographs and doing occasional interviews it would often be time to do the next show.

Once we decided to leave the theatre from a rear door to bypass the autograph seekers. It didn't take long for us to realize that we were making a big mistake. The fans waiting for us had possibly bought our recordings and in a thoughtless move we were running from them. We did this only once after which we signed every piece of paper handed to us.

After all the time we spent in the spotlight we finished what we believed to be a very successful week at the theatre. Fortunately, the Christmas break at Western had given us the opportunity to work a full week without missing a class.

CHAPTER FIFTY

Winter 1952

Frightening words to many new show business personalities are, "IT'S SHOW TIME!" Becoming nervous from hearing this announcement can cause several things to happen: the hands might tremble, voices can get unsteady and worst of all you worry that the talent that got you there might not be accepted by the audience. Critics who'll pay to see and hear you will be expecting first class entertainment. Scary? Not really when you do your best and say, "There you are audience. Take it or leave it."

Such was the case for our foursome when we were booked into Moe's Main Street club in Cleveland. It was our very first job in a night club and we worried that we might not be ready to entertain an audience expecting to see a good show.

A devilish condition that we hoped we would never see is sometimes found in the minds of entertainers. This frightening mindset can cause even the great ones to shrivel and run from the pressure of performing. This mental devil is called stage fright.

Barbara Streisand is an example of a frightened megastar who reportedly suffers from pre-performance fear. In her career of fifty plus years she went three decades refusing to do live performances. After her first late night talk show appearance she went fifty one years before doing another.

Fortunately for our group no one had ever had the tendency to panic at the thought of having to entertain an audience. Nervous? Yes. But that's a temporary condition that usually disappears once the show is underway.

At Moe's Main Street Club, I felt we were the epitome of awkwardness when we stumbled on stage to do our first nightclub show. We were lucky that we didn't fall on our faces before getting to the microphone. Once there we were supposed to sing and do a few simple steps that Jon Gregory had taught us. But nothing was simple as we struggled to keep from making fools of ourselves.

By the third song we had pretty well shaken our nervousness and settled into the routine learned through many hours of practice. The audience seemed pleased with how we performed for about forty minutes. We left the stage relieved that despite some flaws our first club date seemed to have been a success.

On our way to our dressing room a familiar face suddenly appeared from behind one of the tall curtains. To our pleasure we were looking at Jon Gregory, the man who had worked hard to make us look good on stage. Following our greetings to each other he told us that he had flown from New York expressly to see our first show.

Before we could ask, "How'd you like it?" he went straight to the point. Three short words hinted that we needed to shape up something somewhere in our act.

"We gotta' talk," he began. "We're going to go outside to the alley where we can go over some things without disturbing anyone. There are a few steps in your footwork that need to be tightened up and we're going to fix those."

So outside the backdoor we went into the semi-dark alley that would serve as a stage for whatever Jon planned to do to help us.

Once we started our simple footwork routine Jon began counting one and two and three and so on. We were bouncing around with our steps when two drunk passerbys stopped to watch us for a minute or two. They were probably wondering what the heck four grown men were doing dancing next to the garbage cans in a filthy alley. Normally that would have been a valid question. But we knew that what we were doing out there was to ensure that our next show and the ones thereafter would look more professional.

The last show of our appearance at Moe's place was Sunday morning around one o'clock. Just as we were taking our final bow a loud, husky voice rang out above the clapping of the crowd. Plainly understood were the shouter's rousing cheer, "GO KENTUCKY WILDCATS, GO BIG BLUE TEAM!!!"

I had no idea who the enthusiastic screamer was until I got off stage and went out front to meet him. Standing about six-feet-four-inches tall the giant of a man I saw immediately registered in my mind. It was the former All-American football star at the University of Kentucky and presently a starting tackle with the Cleveland Browns, Bob Gain. He and his wife and four other Browns players were having a special night out to come and see the boys from Kentucky perform.

Bob had a broken jaw that had been wired together to hold the injured bones in place. As the kickoff man for the team he said he often tore the wires loose in the strain of kicking. He could eat no solid food but managed to placate himself by watching his wife eat his favorite dishes.

I could tell that Bob's recollections of his college days at Kentucky were still very important to him. I listened to his memories until my three singing buddies got anxious to leave and called me to wrap it up with my friends. I had absolutely no idea that I would be meeting a fine figure of a man who once lived in my home state.

The pleasant week we spent at Moe's Main Street was a good way to hone our act for the club jobs ahead. Doing theatre shows and night spots gave us two different audiences to please. In theatres people are usually quiet and predictably attentive while in most nightclubs someone is forever talking too loud, dropping beer bottles or arguing about last night's football game. The trick of the trade is to learn how to adjust your show to suit whatever audience pays to see you perform.

CHAPTER FIFTY-ONE

During our running from one club or theatre to another, Maxine and I were trying to plan a time when we could get married. We had been going steady for nearly a year after Maxine's friend introduced us in the school cafeteria.

Finding a free day or night was not easy since we were traveling and singing every weekend. We finally decided that after a concert with Lionel Hampton in Youngstown, Ohio we would go to Springfield, Tennessee and quickly but legally tie the knot.

When we got to Springfield we were too late to catch the county clerk in the courthouse. So I called and told him that I would make it worth his while if he would open his office and issue a license to us. I could make it worth his while all right because I was carrying a wad of money that came from being paid in cash in the Youngstown concert. It looked like I was carrying a Coke can in my front pocket.

After paying the clerk handsomely we called a doctor who believed me when I said I would reward him graciously if he would come to his office and give us blood tests. He agreed to come and with the money I gave him for his work he could easily afford to give lots of folks in Springfield free dinners.

First came the license and blood tests. Next, the preacher. The most Reverend Joe Martin welcomed us into his home, performed the ceremony then stuffed a bunch of long green into his pocket. On such a special night I felt that I made at least three people in Springfield very happy by rewarding them handsomely for their services.

On Monday, January 5, 1953, Maxine joined the McGuire family and settled with me in a forty dollars a month rental house in Bowling Green. Life was good. What else could a twenty- one- year old young man want after working in a special world on stage and having a wonderful woman as his wife?

CHAPTER FIFTY-TWO

Phone Conversation
Early 1953

Jimmy: "We're going to have to get together in Washington D.C. one week from today."

Seymour: "Sounds fine. But where's the job, at the downtown theatre or a supper club somewhere?"

Jimmy: "It's not at either of those places. When I tell you where we're going to be I think you'll be shocked."

Seymour: "Shocked? So shock me. What's going to bother us when we've worked every kind of honky tonk known to humankind?"

Jimmy: "Randy is going to be there with us when we sing for the members of the Washington Press Club, their guests from the Pentagon and some of the big dogs from Capitol Hill. I've even heard that the Under Secretary of State is going to be there."

Seymour: "You're kidding."

Jimmy: "No kidding here. Randy has friends in the Press Club so he volunteered us to give a one-half hour show for members and guests at their weekly luncheon."

Seymour: "Well I'll be damned. Never thought we'd have a chance to sing before such an important bunch of people."

One week later we stood in a room just behind the small stage of the main dining area waiting to give our best shot to all the dignitaries out front. Nobody was nervous probably realizing that those who'll hear us won't know a flat note from a goose's quack.

Around one o'clock the apparent spokesman for the Press Club came to the microphone and began the introduction that would bring us on stage. He turned out to be a rather personable MC using his resonating voice to say, "Today, ladies and gentlemen, we have with us four young men who have made quite a mark in the music business. They come from Kentucky and with them they have brought songs that have been hits all over the country! So now Press Club members and guests, let's welcome the group that has been recently named by several polls to be the number one vocal group in America. Let's hear it for — The Hilltoppers!"

Wearing our new blue suits with matching ties we smiled as we came on stage and followed Billy to the small piano where we would stand and sing. Before singing our songs Jimmy stepped forward to express to the audience how honored we were to be invited to such an impressive gathering.

When he finished his short address we prepared to sing when Billy gave us an arpeggio to begin the firs tune. "Trying" started it off. Then came "Love Walked In" with an up beat tempo. Just before beginning our third tune a voice coming surprisingly out of the blue cried loudly, "Come on Hilltoppers! Sing "P.S. I Love You" for us. Do it! Do it!"

Well well, someone out in the large crowd sounded to be aware of our recordings. Whoever yelled was given our appreciation when we sang "P.S." while looking in the direction the request came from.

The final number of our time on stage was "If I Were King", a fast song we had recorded a year or so earlier. Following our final bow, we went off stage to sit with Randy at a special table where we could see and hear the next performers.

Within the next hour or so three very famous composers of popular music played and sang some of the songs they had written over the years. I wish I had written down their names and the songs, many of which reminded me of my growing up years.

The luncheon ended for us when one of the press officials came to our table and thanked us for our performance. Before turning to leave he said to us, "Did you realize that you were singing to two Medal of Honor winners and a commander of an aircraft carrier? And you might want to know that they told me how much they enjoyed your part of the program. I'd say that's quite a compliment."

Supper clubs, college campuses, army bases, television— we thought we'd sung in all the places that books acts for entertainment. But a press club? That was the first and maybe the last such gathering that we would appear before. But with Randy always looking for ways to promote the group there's no telling what other gratis appearances he might have had in mind for us in the future.

CHAPTER FIFTY THREE

Through the Summer of 1953, The Hilltoppers kept doing one-nighters, club dates and an occasional concert with a big band. We were still a hot item in the business, often giving up top money dates to do benefits.

Possibly the most gratifying free show was in Cleveland in July where we sang at a football stadium for the Nurses' Association of Ohio. In our part of the show we were backed with one of the more respected orchestras in the business: Percy Faith's thirty piece ensemble.

After forty or so minutes of singing our biggest hits and other songs came a stage wise duo playing and singing tunes that had made the pop charts. Les Paul and Mary Ford were stars that created a different sound on their guitars and sold millions of records all over the world.

To end the show Percy Faith played his hit song that had captured every music lover's heart. "The Theme from Moulin Rouge" was a beautiful composition played on violins, French horns and every other imaginable instrument. On that warm summer night in a football stadium the sound of those strings drifted gently into and above the crowd, ending the show on a dramatic note.

Another benefit we played was at the War Memorial Auditorium in Nashville. There we sang only two songs, "Trying" and "P.S. I Love You" and were followed by a young singer who was hoping but so far failing to make it in the music business.

Randy, who was there with us, had heard the youngster sing in the past at various functions but hesitated for whatever reason to offer him a recording contract.

Jimmy, our lead singer, suggested to Randy that the newcomer was good enough to take a chance on and record for Dot Records. He finally agreed to Jimmy's suggestion and signed the aspiring singer the following week.

Pat Boone had eight million sellers in a row.

CHAPTER FIFTY FOUR

1953 - The Hot Year

Unknown to most people was the excellent recording studio in the Grand Ol' Opry's Ryman Auditorium. Randy had planned a session for us there where we would record a song that he believed was ready for a comeback. "Till Then", recorded by the Mills Brothers in the early forties, was a tune that never seemed to lose its popularity.

Holding statuettes given for being the Number 1 Vocal Group in America

Randy believed the song would fit Jimmy's solo voice and our vocal backup and have a good chance of making the music charts again. Predictably, the Dot guru was right. Our version of the old hit started a fast run toward the top twenty songs and finally made it to the list of the ten best selling records. So, on the tail of the success of "P.S. I Love You" came another hit for The Hilltoppers.

Our popularity was as strong as it had ever been. And to reward this distinction several of the industry polls voted us the number one vocal group in America. Some of those ranking us as the best in our category were: WNEW, the powerful New York radio station, Cash Box magazine, WERE in Cleveland, the Automatic Coin Industry which kept an accurate account of the number of times a record was played on jukeboxes, Song Hits magazine and several other polls around the country.

As The Hilltoppers' popularity spread across America, answering fan letters and taking phone calls became a growing responsibility. Randy's personal secretary fought this problem for a while but soon admitted that working for both Dot Records and the quartet was too much to handle.

The answer to her problem was only two hours away. Bobbie Ann Mason, a farm girl in Mayfield, Kentucky, had already started a Hilltopper fan club on her own. When the secretary heard of Bobbie Ann's initiative she felt relieved to finally have someone take over the workload she had been handling.

Although Bobbie Ann was only fifteen years old she quickly convinced the secretary, Randy and the quartet that she was capable of handling Hilltopper fan club responsibilities such as contacting disc jockeys and recruiting other teenagers to become regional presidents. As her challenges increased she kept running the club efficiently likes a seasoned professional.

Bobbie Ann and her mother often drove or rode a bus to be with us at performances both close to and often far from their home. Meeting celebrities such as Pat Boone, Eydie Gormé and others made her realize that hoeing corn was not as much fun as being with The Hilltoppers and these stars. While visiting with us in Detroit she was interviewed on TV by comedian Soupy Sales. In this new environment she held her own getting along with the big names she met.

Following graduation from high school Bobbie Ann enrolled at the University of Kentucky and for a while kept running our fan club. In the fall of 1959 The Hilltoppers were scheduled to do a homecoming concert at the university's student center. When we drove into Lexington one of the first things we did was to contact Bobbie Ann at her dormitory.

After meeting with her on campus we asked if she had a date for the dance and concert. When she told us she didn't we assured her she did and that she would be escorted to the festivities by her best friends: the four Hilltoppers.

Our performance, accompanied by the Jimmy Featherstone's band, was one of our best. With their applause fellow Kentuckians in the audience confirmed that we were back on familiar ground in the state where it all started for us.

Bobbie Ann continued to take care of fan club duties for the rest of the year. But with our insistence she finally gave up her club responsibilities, which she had handled like a professional since her mid-teen years.

After leaving the university she worked on and eventually received her PhD in literature. She was to become one of the more recognizable writers in the country. Among her best selling novels was one that would be made into the movie "In Country" starring Bruce Willis. Several times she has been a guest writer for The New Yorker, a magazine that is almost impossible to be featured in. She was slated to be inducted into the Kentucky Hall of Fame for writers who have made significant contributions to the readers of quality literature.

· TOP· ·

Eddie Fisher came out of service to lead the way with one hit tune after another. Records like "Downhearted," "Anytime," "How Do You Speak To An Angel," "Many Times," "I'm Walking Behind You" brought Eddie top honors as the hottest male singer around this past year. Eddie is seen and heard by millions on his own nation-wide television show.

A young gal who, in the short space of one year, has implanted herself on the top rung of the ladder of success is Joni James. Unheard of when her MGM recording of "Why Don't You Believe Me" was released, Joni sold over a million copies of the record and followed up with more of the same, each a big hit.

JONI JAMES—TOP FEMALE STAR

EDDIE FISHER—TOP MALE STAR

★ ★ ★

STARS

A youngster fresh out of the Navy stepped into the Arthur Godfrey show, and before long, Julius LaRosa was a household word. From the Godfrey show he graduated into a top record star on the Cadence label, and now Julie is out on his own, singing to thousands across the country. Definitely one of the bright lights of the year.

A young lady stepped out from the hit Broadway musical revue, "New Faces," to lead the parade of new gal singers and light up the nation's musical hi-lights with a style that was different and a voice that really sold a song. Miss Eartha Kitt and her recording of "C'est Si Bon" took the nation by storm and established a brand new personality.

JULIUS LA ROSA—MOST PROMISING MALE SINGER

EARTHA KITT—MOST PROMISING FEMALE SINGER

★ ★ ★

OF

A group of college kids got together out at Western Kentucky and decided to form a vocal group. Randy Wood of Dot Records heard them and asked them to make a record. The boys did a song called "Trying," and it put them on every phonograph in the country. The Hilltoppers are their name and these boys are here to stay.

The year 1953 was the year for the return of the big band — and leading the way was Capitol's great Ray Anthony, his trumpet, and his ork. Ray introduced a new dance, the Bunny Hop, made the nation "Dragnet"-conscious with a recording of the TV mystery theme, packed every ballroom he appeared in and was the man behind the big band's return.

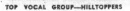

TOP VOCAL GROUP—HILLTOPPERS

1953

TOP BAND—RAY ANTHONY

Wow!!! Looks like we made it!

CHAPTER FIFTY-FIVE

In August of 1953 our group was hit with devastating news. Jimmy was called into the army by his draft board. A bolt of lightning couldn't have hit us any harder. Without Jimmy's fine commercial voice our traveling around the country would have to be put on hold.

So, with no alternative and before Jimmy went into the army, Randy called us together to plan extensive recording sessions that would put a number of songs in reserve to hold us for a while.

What a shocker! And to double our misery, Seymour and I knew that we would be eligible for the draft as soon as we graduated from Western. In a matter of days we went from being successful show business performers to the unemployed ranks. It was such a dramatic change in our lives and we could do nothing to prevent it.

Before Jimmy left we recorded what must have been twenty songs. Jumping into the situation so quickly we wondered if Randy had chosen tunes good enough to measure up to our recordings of the past. If anyone could do it he could.

Following the sessions, Jimmy left for the service spending his first few weeks at Fort Dix, New Jersey. Seymour graduated from Western in the spring of 1953 and I received my diploma at mid-term 1954. What a shame that when we were rolling at top speed in the music business personal appearances came to an abrupt halt.

Accepting the fact that we were off the road for at least two years, I finally found time to pay more attention to my here-to-fore neglected wife.

From Friday until Monday morning Maxine had been staying alone in our rental house. It had been rare for me to be with her over the weekend.

As far as spreading The Hilltopper name in person, those days were gone for a while. Now we had to wait and hope that during the time we were out of action the recordings would keep us in the public's ears. And surprisingly they did.

"The Kentuckian Song", a movie soundtrack tune, made it into the top fifteen list of hits. "To Be Alone" landed in the number twelve slot and "Love Walked In" scored in the top twenty category. These weren't smash hits but at least we were keeping our name alive through their releases.

In the meantime Randy had made a decision to move Dot Records to California. The company, which had never had a hit record until we recorded "Trying" had grown dramatically. Pat Boone continued to be a hot item. The Fontane Sisters of the Perry Como show had a few hits, Jim Lowe sold a bunch of recordings of "Green Door" and other artists sold enough records for Randy to get an offer of several million dollars for Dot Records from Paramount Pictures. After the move he was to remain president of Dot and vice president of Paramount. What a change this was for a company that had its first big hit only four years earlier.

CHAPTER FIFTY-SIX

Spring 1954

During the months following my graduation, Maxine and I moved into a sixty-dollars a month rental house. Now we were really standing tall. Since our final tour in 1953, I had very little to do in the music business. However, Seymour and I often contacted Randy to stay abreast of what was going on with Dot.

The company was rapidly expanding, especially after signing Tab Hunter (not a good singer) and Gayle Storm (a much better one) both of whom had a number of big hits. Randy, always looking for new talent, used the name value of the two movie stars and other well known Hollywood actors to sell records. His very shrewd business mind kept him on top of the competition.

Meanwhile, Maxine and I took a belated honeymoon trip to Florida. It was belated because after our Springfield, Tennessee marriage we spent our one honeymoon night in a Nashville motel. The Florida trip made up for having only one brief night to celebrate our marriage.

On our way home from Florida we drove to Moulton, Alabama to attend the wedding of Seymour and Jeanne Warren. We met Randy, his wife, Lois, and Al Bennett there for what turned out to be a reunion of sorts. With one-half of the Hilltoppers missing, however, things just weren't the same.

Once back in Bowling Green, Maxine and I were happy to settle in our sixty dollar a month mansion. After unpacking I went through our large accumulation of mail. The usual bills were in the stack but one letter seemed out of place. It was from Washington D.C. When I opened it the first word I saw gave me a strong clue as to what the letter was about.

"Greetings" it began. The remainder of the letter informed me that Uncle Sam needed my services. In short, I had been drafted and instructed to be at a certain place at a certain time to begin my two-year commitment.

Even though I knew that calling me into active duty was imminent, I was still shocked by the official induction paper. And without my being aware of it, Seymour also received his "Greetings". Now three-fourths of our group were serving our country, losing more income than a calculator could register. What had become a very lucrative business for us during the past two years of performing was now bankrupt.

After two months of basic training I was accepted into special services but was released along with all the assigned soldiers when the commanding officer was caught stealing whiskey and money. Following that debacle, I spent six weeks in clerical school learning how to type then was ordered to Baltimore to begin duty as a company clerk. I moved Maxine from Bowling Green to live off post with me near my base. I was stationed in a small unit one mile from Pimlico racetrack which was obviously not a typical military post.

CHAPTER FIFTY-SEVEN

In the Spring of 1955 Jimmy was discharged from the army and immediately formed an interim Hilltopper quartet. He auditioned several singers in New York and finally hired two excellent vocalists to work with him on the road. Eddie Crowe, from Jimmy's hometown, also joined the group as the baritone voice and added his talent to the sound of the quartet. Other than being a fine singer, he played jazz piano, the trumpet and did impressions of various famous people. I saw the act only once just before re-joining the group and thanked the powers that be, they no longer wore those dadburn beanies.

Early in December Seymour and I took our rightful places back into the quartet. It was a different scene than we left two years earlier. Our records were still being played but were selling only so-so. What we needed was another hit to get us high on the charts again. Three of four releases of the past few months had not done well and Randy was unhappy with himself for not finding a song with hit potential.

Around the same time we were combing publishing houses for good songs to record. A different sound was coming out of most recording studios. This new music form had its beginning in Cleveland, Ohio in 1951 and had slowly grown in popularity with the teenagers. The music wasn't pop as we knew it and it wasn't traditional blues or country. We really didn't know what it was.

The lesser talented musicians played and sang a maximum three chords and terribly poor lyrics that were often difficult to understand. Melodies were sung mostly by youngsters who didn't know a music key from a door key. We were to learn that this unusual music was being called Rock n' Roll.

The music was so repulsive to a great percentage of the general public that some radio stations put bans on it. Many churches rebelled against it. Lovers of the "good ol' music" were angry because their pop and traditional music were taking a beating.

Why did so many young people take such a liking to it? Why did they abandon the music their parents had tried to pass on to them? Answers to those questions vary. However, the one that seems to hit the target was that the 1950s generation had tired of hearing about the depression, World War II and the Korean police action. They had heard enough of the troubled past and its old music. Rock n' Roll was theirs and they were determined to hang with it.

CHAPTER FIFTY-EIGHT

Shortly before I was discharged Maxine gave birth to our first child, whom we named Cynthia Lea McGuire. Of course the name Cynthia soon became Cindy.

Maxine had been through a tough labor and was anxious to get back to our apartment where she could rest in familiar surroundings. Before leaving the hospital one of the nurses advised us to keep the car warm while driving home. We took her advice but added a bit more heat than she recommended. When we got to the apartment you could fry an egg on the dashboard. Maxine was sweating, I was sweating while newborn Cindy was peacefully asleep. One thing I learned about our car that day was that it had a helluva heater.

CHAPTER FIFTY-NINE

January 1957

Being popular in the entertainment world can bring a variety of show people to your door asking for favors. This was the case when Randy, Al Bennett and the four of us were playing Tonk and relaxing in the Warwick Hotel in New York before a recording session.

Around three o'clock in the afternoon, the phone rang and Randy answered it hearing the caller say, "Mr. Wood, Mr. Milton Berle is here in the lobby and would like to meet with you in your suite if you could arrange it."

Randy asked the caller to hold for a second then turned to us and asked, "Do we want to talk to Milton Berle right now? He's in the lobby hoping to come up and try to persuade us to record a song he's written. He's bothered me before about this so I guess I should see him and get this thing out of the way."

In a flash I thought, "We're in the position of telling the most famous man on TV to go jump in the lake." But I knew that wasn't about to happen. Randy was too much of a gentleman to be rude and turn Mr. Berle away.

Ten minutes later we met the television star just before he began making his pitch to Randy. In less than five minutes Randy effected a trade with our visitor. In the agreement Jimmy would do a single of Milton's tune and we would have a spot on his show to sing our latest recording.

It all worked out well so we settled back into our card game. Ho hum. Just another day at the office.

CHAPTER SIXTY

When Randy Wood moved Dot Records to California his sales manager, Al Bennett, decided he would cash in his ten percent ownership of the company. Al had been a devoted Dot employee and a good friend of our group. However, he was the worst golfer I had ever seen, drove his car ninety miles an hour through town and played poker till all hours of the night. Despite his hyperactive lifestyle he managed to be at every Hilltopper recording session.

After we said our goodbyes to Al he took his ten percent (reportedly a healthy sum) and bought part of Liberty Records in Los Angeles. He was there only a short time when he and his two partners had a huge hit record called "Witch Doctor". Other hits followed and in only a few months Al had added a substantial amount of dollars to his bank account.

One evening when he and his partners were in the recording studio they decided to experiment and speed up the tape that had three male voices on it. When it ended Al asked his friends what the voices sounded like and one of them said, "It sounds like little animals of some description but what kind of animals?"

After a minute or two of racking their brains Al volunteered that he thought he had an appropriate name to go with their new discovery.

"Tell me what you think about these little creatures. They're very small, dig a bunch of holes in our yards and are just about impossible to catch in a trap. How about 'The Chipmunks'," Al suggested. "How does that sound to you?"

Without hesitating, one of the partners said, "Yeah, that's perfect but now we have to decide what we're going to name each one."

The third partner then asked the simple question, "Al, your legal name has to be what? Alvin?"

"Yeah, that's it," Al confirmed.

"Then we have a natural here. The name Alvin is going to be IT for the leader of the group."

"And if I might suggest," Al said. "You, Simon, will put your name on one of them and Theodore, the long form of Ted, will go with the third one. How does that sound?"

"Sounds fine," Simon replied. "Now we have three new friends in our company and from now on they'll be called 'Alvin and the Chipmunks'."

So when I hear the familiar voices of the Chipmunks at Christmas or a anytime I can proudly claim that Alvin is a friend of mine.

Incidentally, Al made his final business deal in the record industry by selling his company for thirty-eight million dollars. Sadly, he passed away when in his mid-sixties.

CHAPTER SIXTY-ONE

February 1957

Over the past five years we had worked with so many talented and well known performers. At the Michigan State Fair the bill was filled with stars such as Johnny Ray, Eydie Gorme, Bill Haley and The Comets, Guy Mitchell, Billy Ward and The Dominoes and several other recognizable names. It was the largest collection of show people with which we had ever shared a stage.

Following the Michigan show I was anxious to get to our new home in Owensboro and to Maxine, who was close to having our second child. Jimmy, Seymour and Doug were going south for a brief vacation so on their way they dropped me off at the Daviess County Hospital in Owensboro.

On February 10, Donald Kreis McGuire, Jr. became a welcomed member of our family. Maxine thought he was the cutest baby she had ever seen. I thought he looked like Elvis Presley. Regardless of his looks he was a fine and healthy ten pound baby boy.

Back on the road again we were happy to be playing more and more college concerts where we always found some of our best audiences. Like the few Armed Forces shows we did they would laugh at most anything and respond well to our songs.

At Camp Perry just outside Toledo, Ohio we did a show with Tony Bennett who was just getting started in the business. As expected, the soldiers made our day by responding to Hilltopper songs that might have been popular during their high school years.

Mr. Bennett was also well received, especially when he sang his smooth rendition of "Because Of You" . Of course we had no idea that he would become such a super star in the music business. But with his very recognizable style and voice quality he was sure to become a top performer.

During the next four months we followed a schedule that took us over a lot of territory. Once, after a concert deep in Nebraska (Kearney State Teachers College), our booking agent called and told us that he had made a mistake in his Hilltopper appearance schedule. He neglected to notify us that we were due to be in Cincinnati by three o'clock the following day for a band rehearsal at the Castle Farms Ballroom. From Kearney to Cincinnati had to be a jillion miles. The question was could we make it?

With no airport in Kearney, we had no choice but to turn our big Fleetwood toward Ohio and let it eat up the miles. To our surprise we made it in time for the band rehearsal. After finishing there, we called our agent and told him to take and stick his faulty booking schedule notes where it's very dark.

Another marathon trip we made that had us traveling all night was from Midland, Texas to El Paso. I didn't think we'd ever get there. It was a bunch of miles to cover to do one show at the town's civic center. But we did it, then told our agent that he should start booking us with travel of not more than four hundred miles a day. I don't think he heard our plea.

CHAPTER SIXTY-TWO

In the mid-fifties one of the biggest stars in the recording industry was Johnny Ray. For approximately three years he scored hit after hit and was ranked by several polls as America's bestseller of single records in the country.

We got to know Johnny at the Michigan State Fair. Each act had its own mobile home to rest in and change clothes for the session in which they would perform. To kill time between shows Seymour, Eddie, Johnny and I usually played bridge until it was our turn to do our minutes on stage. When time came for Johnny's second show of the day I told him I wanted to be out front to catch his act which I hadn't had a chance to see.

One hour later I took a good seat halfway to the back of the auditorium and waited for our bridge partner to hit the stage and do what he does best. Finally the show's public address announcer gave Johnny a flowery intro ending with, "And now, here he is. America's favorite songster. Let's say hello to Mr. Johnny Ray!!"

The moment he said "Ray" Johnny burst through the curtain and began singing, "Gee but it's great after stayin' out late, walkin' my baby back home." It was one of his hit songs currently ranking high on the popularity charts. Four songs later he sat down at the piano and began playing the first part of the introduction to his next song. Then speaking to the audience in a soft voice said, "The song I'm about to sing is a favorite of my mother and dad. And each night I dedicate it to them because I know how much they love it. The song is called, 'The Little White Cloud That Cried.'

Thirty minutes later we're back at the bridge table and I'm congratulating him for doing a fine show. Then I made it a point to tell him how much I was impressed by his dedicating "The Little White Cloud That Cried" to his parents. It was indeed a thoughtful thing to do.

He looked at me with a wry little grin and much to my surprise said, "Hell, they've never heard it. That's all done for show."

"Don't tell me that," I said. "I don't want to hear it. Tell me you're putting me on."

"Can't do that," he returned. "It keeps the audience in love with me. Remember it's called show business."

"You rascal," I teased. "You'll do anything to get the crowd with you, won't you?"

"Yep, almost anything. As long as the band keeps backing me."

Probably our biggest disappointment in a band came when we were booked to do a concert in a regional Kentucky college.

The rehearsal was set for four o'clock with the show scheduled to begin three hours later. When we walked into the concert hall we could hear the band practicing one of the better known standards, "Stardust". Their horns were in tune, the drummer was on beat and the piano player sounded professional. From what we heard, we hoped our arrangements would be played as well as they were playing theirs. After introducing ourselves we began passing out our arrangements of fifteen songs to the appropriate sections. Once finished, Eddie, who would direct the band's rehearsal, gave instructions regarding our opening song.

"Okay, listen up," Eddie began. "We'll come on stage when you begin playing, 'I Feel A Song Coming On'. Please notice that the song is to be played in a bright two-four time. It's critical that we get the tempo right in the opener. Okay?"

The band's director acknowledged Eddie's instructions then turned to face his band with a peculiar look on his face. Eddie had no idea why the man seemed to be very nervous.

"All right, I'm going to give you a two-for-nothing kickoff and then we'll play. (A two-for-nothing kickoff means counting 1-2, 1-2 then start playing.)

"Okay, let's get ready to do it," Eddie alerted, lifting his hand high to give the downbeat.

"Ready. Here we go. One-two-one-two play."

One trumpet, a trombone and the piano were the only instruments that could be heard attempting to play the opener. The remaining ten players played not a single note. Eddie was stunned.

"Are all of us on the same page? It's 'I Feel A Song Coming On'. Is that what your arrangement says?"

"Yes sir, that's what it says but the tempo is too fast," a saxophone player volunteered. "We have a tough time with arrangements that go as fast as this one. I wish I didn't have to tell you that."

"So do I," Eddie said under his breath. "Okay, if we can't handle that one let's go to the second song, 'Till Then'. It's in four-four time with a slow tempo. You should be able to read that one. Let's do it—-one—-two—-three—-four, play," Eddie began the count.

What came out of the instruments were only weak attempts to read the notes even in the slow tempo.

When the band struggled through the thirty-two measures and finished, Eddie was livid as he thought, "How could whoever is in charge of this damn concert give us such a rotten band?"

But instead of continuing to feel terribly disappointed he righted himself and sweated through every note the band attempted to play.

When the final tune ended, Eddie was a wreck. The way the band read or didn't read the music was going to make for a lousy show and he knew it. His final message to the musicians was, "Be sure you play softly and if you get lost then play only the melody if you know it. Don't worry about reading our arrangements."

Jimmy, Seymour and I had been listening to the rehearsal from the rear of the auditorium. Like Eddie, we were having a tough time thinking that a full house was going to have to listen to this band.

It was six thirty, one half hour from show time and we were dreading getting dressed and fighting our way through ninety-five minutes of performing.

Somehow, someway we made it to the finish after singing in front of the large audience. As expected, the band was lousy but we managed to entertain the crowd without making any major goofups.

Our motto when we thought for whatever reason that we'd done a less than average show was, "Get the loot and scoot."

But that night after singing with a poor band we were surprised when one of the ticket holders came to us and said, "That was a great show you just put on. Maybe we can have you back here sometime in the near future." Others followed with similar compliments.

The four of us nearly fainted.

We left town completely exhausted from the stress that came from performing with the worst band we'd ever worked with.

CHAPTER SIXTY-THREE

April 1957

When we were interviewed on radio and TV the first question invariably asked was, "How did you guys get together?" And near the end of most interviews another familiar inquiry was usually, "When did you know when you'd made it big in the business?"

Answering the first question usually became my responsibility. For some reason Jimmy, Seymour and Billy (when he was traveling with us) backed away from the microphone, leaving me there to answer the disc jockey's questions. I actually think they took naps while I was wearing out my brain out trying to satisfy the curious interviewers.

When Billy was asked a question in a radio interview he usually answered with a shake or nod of his head. Predictably the DJ would say, "Billy, if you don't mind, we're not on television. What do you think about my last question?" To be cute Billy would often reply, "What question?"

There were several times and events in our early days in the business that made us feel we had reached star status. Once in New York when we were getting ready to do the Patty Page NBC TV show, Maxine and I took a walk to Times Square just to relax for an hour or so. In those days the record shops opened their doors and windows to let the sound of their best selling records be heard by passerbys. We couldn't keep from feeling extra proud when we heard virtually every shop we passed blasting out The Hilltoppers' "P.S. I Love You". We were hearing the third ranked song in

America making a sweet sound in midtown Manhattan. A man from the hills of Eastern Kentucky in Times Square—now that ain't too bad.

When Maxine and I were seeing the New York sights we were only four hours away from doing Patty Page's TV show. To couple with hearing our song being played in Times Square, we were highly honored to be working the show in, of all great places, Radio City. No chopped liver here. It was and still is one of the more important venues for performing entertainers to play. To top off a memorable day, our appearance on the show went great.

Another time we felt that we were on a hot roll was when we were invited to watch the Perry Como show live at CBS. Our personal manager, Jack Spina and Mr. Como's best friend, had told us that Perry was going to sing our "To Be Alone" as his last number on the show and he wanted us to be there to hear his rendition.

When he started and finished the song and went off the air, he asked the audience and the orchestra to stay seated for a few minutes. He wanted to introduce them to the singers who made popular his final song on the show.

Following our introduction he asked us to come up on the stage and back him when he sang our song one more time. We anticipated that the next few minutes were going to be less than professional.

We were right. As we approached him he said in sort of phony sarcastic voice, "Okay, you guys who thought you were so hot recording the song I just finished, get behind me. You can do the humming while I solo it again."

The audience, sensing that something out of character for Perry was happening, laughed lightly waiting for what he planned to do or say next.

"Okay, Mitch, let's do it," he said to his music director Mitchell Ayres. From the beginning of the tune things started getting crazy. He was singing but we were starting to act foolish behind him, looking cross-eyed and making faces.

Around the middle of the song I did the unmentionable. I goosed him on his rear end with my thumb making him flinch as he swayed from side to side.

The crowd, seeing what had happened, began laughing and so did we. Then suddenly I began realizing what I'd done and said to myself,

"What in the hell am I doing? I've just punched one of the greatest popular singers in the world in the fanny in front of five hundred people. What have I done?"

I hoped what I did would be taken in good faith by Perry.

After he finished singing the song he turned to us with a wide smile and said, "It was great having you guys here to do a little cutting up. Thanks for coming."

Not one word was said about the goosing and I was tickled to no end there wasn't.

To me that evening of fooling around with a huge star helped reinforce the fact that we were riding high in the business. It would always be a special night for The Hilltoppers to remember.

Perry Como was the nicest person we worked with in the entertainment business.

CHAPTER SIXTY-FOUR

One of our more pleasant jobs was working a fine supper club known as Fazio's on Fourth in Milwaukee. It was located in the center of the city's shopping district across the street from the largest hotel in town.

Staying in the hotel at the time were players with the famous New York Yankee baseball team. Their exhibition game with the Milwaukee Braves was scheduled for the following day in the Brave's new stadium.

The members of the Yankee team were famous celebrities showing their skills in front of millions of people each year. One of the more pleasant moments in the entertainment business was meeting people like some of the Yankees who had become famous but refused to let success go to their heads. Of course a perfect example of being famous with no nose stuck up in the air was our friend Perry Como. And there were many others.

Being humble and famous at the same time are not limited to people in show business. For example, when some of the Yankees came into Fazio's, most were smiling, shaking hands and even giving autographs to fans who asked for them.

Everywhere they played a game most of these players were often besieged by autograph seekers. Of course some of them perceived themselves as being the star-of-stars, refusing to bow low and sign a piece of paper.

Such was not the case for one of the Yankees. This very recognizable player was looking for a place where he could get away from the smoke and whiskey in the supper club's main dining room. He was allergic to cigarette and cigar smoke and cringed when anyone lit tobacco close to him.

To escape the acrid smell of the dining room Yogi Berra stopped at our dressing area and asked if he could watch our TV set until his friends finished eating their dinners.

After a quick recovery from seeing who was asking a favor, we said hello to one of the better catchers in the history of major league baseball. He was famous and from what we had heard here and there was a very humble man. Seymour replied to his request to use our room and watch TV.

"Mr. Berra we—

"It's Yogi. Please call me Yogi."

"Okay Yogi. We're going to go on stage in about ten minutes so why don't you have a seat in our dressing room and watch all the television you care to."

"You sure you won't mind?" Yogi asked. "I promise I won't bother a thing and when you come back I'll go upstairs to my friends."

"Sounds fine," Seymour approved. "We're going to do our show now and should be back in less than one hour. Okay?"

"Yeah, that's more than okay," Yogi added. "Hope things go right for you up there on the stage."

We sang our songs for the better part of one hour and finished with applause confirming that we had pleased our audience. With the ever present sweating from being under super bright lights, we were always ready and anxious to hurry back to our dressing room and change into dry clothes.

When we opened the door to where we dressed, we saw Yogi sitting in front of the TV watching no serious acting show, ballgame or news channel. He seemed mesmerized by the cartoons he had probably been watching since we left him.

When he heard us come in the door he turned and said, "Well, how did it go? Did you have a good audience?"

I answered him in the affirmative and asked him how his hour went watching television.

"Oh, it was just fine. I can't tell you how great it was getting away from that stinking dining room," he said as he got up from his chair. "Now I best be getting back to my buddies upstairs. They're going to think I got lost or something. But before I go let me thank you for letting me use your room for a little while. You were nice to do what you did."

We said our goodbyes and watched him climb the steps leading to the main floor. We couldn't keep from thinking what a nice man we had visiting with us. If I could have made one request of him to do something special for me, I would probably have asked, "May I meet Mickey Mantle?"

CHAPTER SIXTY-FIVE

In late August 1957, Randy was alerted to an unusually commercial song written and sung by a young artist in New England. Acting quickly, he called and told us that we were going to cover a cute tune called "Marianne". Cover of course meant that we were going to try to out sell the originator of the song with our recording.

Two weeks later the song by The Hilltoppers was on record and the usual promotion for a new release was set in motion. It looked good during the first four weeks after release and even better the second month when it reached number two on the national charts. "Marianne" was being sung or hummed by kids six years old and adults of all ages. It was a huge seller, making all of us believe that we were back on top again.

We weren't. Rock n' Roll had become king of the record industry and groups like ours were slowly losing the young record buyers' attention. The Four Lads, The Mills Brothers, The Ames Brothers, The Four Freshman and several other groups of our vintage were losing the battle to dominate the rating charts. We were called transition groups meaning that our popularity had come between the older music and the new rage, Rock n' Roll. Now we had to accept the fact that the young people of this country had found a music form they could call their own.

We tried to join the trend and record a few Rock songs. They were so easy to sing but record buyers knew that we weren't a rock group and paid little attention to our offerings. The last recording by us that made a few waves was called "The Joker". It made the charts around the number twenty mark but that was it.

CHAPTER SIXTY-SIX

To describe a typical Hilltopper recording session I would have to use the words tense, educational, frustrating and fun. Certain people in our group made the three hour sessions entertaining and funny with some of their wacky goings on.

The worst member of the recording team to bring mischief into the studio was Billy Vaughn. He was always looking to ease the mild tension usually found early in the session.

Once in a Hollywood studio he had made only one copy of his arrangement for Seymour, Eddie and me to read from. The beginning of the song was okay, but as we approached the bridge the notes kept getting higher and higher making each of us strain to sing the chords.

"Hold it. Hold it," Eddie said loudly. "Billy, how in the hell can we sing notes so high that a soprano would have trouble reaching. I think I got a hernia on the last few chords."

"Yeah, maybe you're right, Eddie," Billy admitted. "But before we throw it out let's try it one more time to make sure it's out of our ranges. Okay?"

"Yeah," Eddie responded halfheartedly. "One more time."

At Billy's direction the band kicked off the introduction to the tune and we began singing our parts again. After a few seconds we were coming to the notes that gave us trouble in our first attempt to sing them. Once there, the three of us leaned backward toward the floor trying to hit the same high notes that we fought on the first take.

At the apex of our misery I smelled paper burning and jumped when I and the other two saw flames coming from the bottom of our arrangement sheet. Billy who had concocted the series of tough notes to sing had set fire to his paper creation. The tune we had planned to record was cancelled because of high notes that if reached would probably have given the three of us very large hernias.

More proof that Billy was a jokester came when he pulled a stunt on me after we finished recording a pretty tune.

I was still a smoker in the late 1950's. So was Billy. We once lit up together when our session took a short break before wrapping it up for the night. Billy finished his smoke then reached over and took the cigarette from my hand. Like an idiot he stuck it in his mouth for a second then handed it back to me with the fire extinguished. He pulled the same trick on Eddie who was sitting next to us.

"Billy, what in the world are you trying to do?" I asked my nutty friend "That's the dumbest trick I've ever seen."

"Oh, I don't know," he replied. "I guess I just wanted to save you the trouble of snuffing out your cigarette. If you'll light another one I'll be glad to kill the fire again for you."

Recording songs on tape in a studio is serious business. However, to keep things from getting too uptight we could always count on Billy to put smiles on our faces.

Some of the more enjoyable moments of a recording session came from working with great musicians and I mean great. During one of our breaks I can remember listening to the piano and guitar players doing an impromptu casual riff. They had just finished accompanying us and were now using their break time improvising on a popular tune.

The fingers of the guitar player were absolutely flying over the frets and the piano player was staying with him with his super quick fingering.

When they finished their brief duet I asked one of our studio technicians who the two men were. He answered, "You've probably never heard of either one of them but believe me, they are two of the best players you'll ever hear. The guitar player is Benny Castle who was just voted the best jazz player in the world."

"The gentleman playing the piano is not widely known but by most critics he's considered the finest keyboard player in Los Angeles. His name is Tommy Brown."

"Well, if they're so good why are they playing on this session instead of making personal appearances somewhere?" I asked the technician.

"Easy answer. Both are married with children so they have no desire to leave them and hit the road to entertain audiences. As you know, they're making good money for this and many other sessions they play in town. They're satisfied with accompanying different artists and staying at home."

I thanked the technician for answering my question then sat and quietly listened to two fine musicians continuing to improvise on their break.

CHAPTER SIXTY-SEVEN

October 1957

When we were in New York we always stayed at the Warwick Hotel. Jack Spina, our and Pat Boone's personal manager had told us that most of the stage actors and visiting movie stars made the hotel their second home.

It wasn't unusual to see Bob Hope, Clark Gable and other notable residents come through the lobby on their way in or out.

Maxine had become aware of this and often lingered lobbyside in hopes of catching one or more of the stars passing through. She was having no luck in her wait so to give her some company I sat with her for a few minutes.

Late in the afternoon when the lobby was getting busy I saw her suddenly come within a hair of fainting when she saw charismatic Burt Lancaster walk in the front door. I think she went into rigor mortis as she stared a hole through him. Later she told me that she was flirting with paralysis when Burt gave her a quick smile and friendly nod.

I really believe that Maxine would have pitched a tent on the lobby's soft carpet if she thought she might catch more notables walking close to her.

CHAPTER SIXTY-EIGHT

In June 1958, we made arrangements to fly to England for a two-month engagement in eight different cities. More shows would be added to our schedule that would take us to Edinburgh and Glasgow, Scotland. The work in what was called "Variety" theatres gave us lots of spare time before doing two early evening shows.

Seymour and I often lived in what were called theatrical digs. These private homes gave us an idea of what residential living in England was all about. The homes were attractive but most had appliances that would look primitive in America. We couldn't help but notice their outdated TV sets, small but functioning refrigerators with no freezers and fireplaces furnishing the only heat in the house.

Despite these differences there was always a fine relationship between us and the people who allowed us to stay in their homes.

There were many attractions for us to enjoy in England. Being typical American tourists, we went to Westminster Abbey, the jewel house holding the country's precious stones, Madame Tussaud's famous wax museum and other sights that were interesting to see for the first time.

To me the food was lousy. Beef sandwiches had a slice of meat about as thick as a newspaper's front page on hard bread that a hammer couldn't break. But to top it all I ate red pudding without knowing that it had been made from pork blood. Yuck and double yuck. The locals loved the stuff but I know I would throw up if I even thought about eating another service of pig blood.

We managed to survive on England's traditional cuisine as we made our way around the country on their highly efficient railroad system. The trains ran on time when leaving and arriving at stations. Each stop was timed to near perfection.

Usually riding the trains with us were supporting acts who did their performances thirty minutes or so before we came on. They were good at their trades and were very professional, practicing their routines every morning at the theatre.

The most unusual act that worked with us for two or three weeks was the dart blowing team. They did exactly what their name suggests. The husband blew darts at balloons attached to a board ten feet away from where he stood. His wife courageously sat among the balloons as the darts popped each one close to her torso. What an act!

After working for one month in England we found ourselves growing a bit weary from being away from home so long. And we still had one month to go before finishing our theatre work. The June weather had been wet and cold but July's nice days with comfortable temperatures gave us chances to play golf (with rented clubs of course) and spend more time outdoors.

One of the special days for us was in a recording studio in London. Our British agent had found a beautiful tune that hadn't been recorded by any English singer.

It was a mystery to everyone why none of the song hustlers in England missed the boat on this tune. It was rare for these special people to overlook a new and beautiful song certain to be a big seller. But they did miss and we were fortunate to have landed such a gem to record. It was simply too pretty to be tucked away in some publishing house file.

"Welcome To My Heart." We recorded this song in a London studio with every instrument known to the music world—strings, oboes, flutes, French horns, trumpets, trombones all added up to twenty-five pieces backing us.

With top promotion the record might have sold one hundred copies. Maybe. We couldn't give it away. It didn't make sense that the public would reject such a classic tune.

Using elaborate instrumentation and top notch arranging on this song didn't work. Comparing this session to our first one it seems unlikely that only four voices and a piano could sell three quarters of a million records. There's no way to explain it.

CHAPTER SIXTY-NINE

After finishing performances in Bristol, Sheffield and Manchester, we went back to London and Finsbury Park Theatre to wind up our tour. The reception there was great. In most theatres we had worked the crowds had been average in attendance. But at Finsbury it was different. Monday through Thursday the audiences filled more than three-fourths of the theatre. And on the weekend they were even bigger, especially at the eight o'clock show. The place was packed Friday and Saturday.

Eight weeks and ninety-six shows in Scotland and England finished what we considered to be a successful run in the theatres we worked. But now it was time to make a full turn toward home and try to re-establish ourselves with our families.

Many times while in England I thought about Maxine and what a task it was for her to run our household and tend to the children at the same time. I kept remembering the responsibilities, small or large, that she faced every day: paying the bills, running off encyclopedia salesmen, cutting the grass, preparing meals and on and on. I don't know how she did it.

Was this arrangement fair to her? I asked myself that question many times always answering "no". She didn't agree with my feeling guilty but instead kept encouraging me to hang in and keep bringing money home in big bags. Someday I would finish traipsing around the world and come home to the ones closest to me. I wondered how much longer that would be.

Getting on the airplane at five o'clock in the afternoon felt extra good because I knew the next stop was going to be home: the good ol' United

States. I don't remember how long the flight took with piston engines but I do recall that we lost one of them halfway across the ocean. It was the first time in all our travels that we had witnessed an engine failure and we sweated it out like all the other passengers.

I think people on board felt much better when the Captain's voice came over the PA system assuring that the plane had ample power to make it to New York. Turning toward Newfoundland to land was not necessary. I'm certain that the people were relieved to hear that we weren't in any danger of taking a bath in the Atlantic Ocean.

Home. What a wonderful feeling it was to walk in the front door after being in foreign countries for two months. I think it was the best hug I'd ever had from Maxine. Sixty days without being with her or seeing the beautiful little rascals standing beside her were now history. What a great feeling!

The next few days at home I didn't think very much of what was coming next for the quartet. I knew we would probably be back on the road again within ten days or so where the routine would start all over again.

Despite a few brief negative thoughts, I had to admit that entertaining people lit up the four of us like Roman candles. On stage, under the brightest lights, big thumping band playing our arrangements, people reacting to what we were doing—how could I not get the special feeling that most people would never have the chance to experience. I was very fortunate to be doing what I was doing.

CHAPTER SEVENTY

After we worked the Holiday House supper club in Pittsburgh in 1958 Eddie decided that he was going to fulfill a dream and become a standup comedian. When he left us we had to find a replacement to sing the baritone voice. Joking, we had a policy stating that in order to become a Hilltopper the hiree must be able to do two things: fit into the tuxedo of the departing singer and guarantee to drive four hundred miles without bitching.

It so happened that Seymour's brother-in-law in school at Western was a capable singer and an excellent trumpet player. Doug Cardoza, a handsome, Portuguese ex-Navy man was going to be asked to join the group and be ready to rehearse his parts with us at Western. Doug had never dreamed that someday he would be jumping into show business with a top singing group. Despite the pressure he must have felt he seemed to handle all the new music and limited choreography very well.

Students who had heard we were on campus were welcomed to watch us work with Doug in the music building. Sometimes there were as many as fifty watching us push him around to practice his stage movements. Learning twenty songs wasn't easy but Doug's music training helped him read notes in all the songs.

Finally it was Showtime for Doug as a singing Hilltopper. Our first job with him was at Birmingham Southern College and the second at Memphis State University. He looked great on stage but we had to nudge him every now and then with our elbows to put him in the right spots at the right time. Predictably, he handled his initiation into show business without a major hitch.

CHAPTER SEVENTY-ONE

October 1958

The toughest job we worked was in Las Vegas at the now defunct Nevada Club. To begin our work night we ate breakfast, watched a late movie then did our first performance at midnight. For one month we did six shows a night in the lounge adding up to one- hundred-forty-four stage appearances in thirty days. During our final show of the night the sun was coming up.

At the end of each week we had one day off. Every Sunday we ate breakfast with Howie Morris, the actor who later became my favorite character on the Andy Griffith show. He played one of the more unforgettable roles as Ernest T. Bass. I was surprised to learn later that he acted in only five episodes of the show in 1963 and 1964. I wished he had been in all of them. He also directed several episodes.

Our second toughest job was in Texas and New Mexico. The Furr Supermarket chain gave free tickets to our show if customers bought a certain amount of groceries. We did twelve straight one-nighters often driving all night. Riding their bus each day and night was the famous Jimmy Dorsey band. I called the vehicle the "iron lung" because of the close quarters on the inside.

The other acts in the traveling show were Julius LaRosa, Herb Shriner of early television, the Decastro sisters (Teach Me Tonight) and of course the fine Dorsey band. The tour became a physical challenge often pushing us to drive up to four hundred miles a day.

Covering those miles with us was the cowboy star Rex Allen who was courting Babette of the DeCastro sisters. True to form, Rex wore his cowboy hat everywhere he went.

To kill time before the shows, he, Julius LaRosa, Seymour and I sometimes played two-on-two basketball using a tennis ball to shoot at a roughly rounded coat hanger basket nailed to a wood post. Our court was no Madison Square Garden but the games we played were important in filling time before it was our turn to go on stage.

CHAPTER SEVENTY-TWO

Tom Fox, a Furr Supermarket manager traveling with us, called for the company's single engine airplane to be brought to him once each week. Members of our tour group were invited to fly one act at a time to the next show site. Seymour and I volunteered to be passengers on the next flight heading for Denver and our next concert.

At 2:00 P.M. the pilot, Tom, and two Hilltoppers took off from Roswell, New Mexico on what was to be a four hour flight to Denver. The weather was perfect with no wind or clouds in the area. The sky held a deep shade of blue as we took off and headed for our assigned altitude.

An hour or so into the flight, I noticed patches of fog as we passed them on both sides of the plane. Visibility suddenly went from good to fair and the sun disappeared into the clouds.

At the time none of us, including the pilot, were paying serious attention to the fickle weather condition around us. But thirty minutes later things began to change. Visibility went from fair to limited and suddenly we were blindly encased in thick clouds.

To compound a bad situation, the pilot turned to Seymour and me and said loudly above the engine's noise, "LOOKS LIKE WE'RE GOING TO HAVE A SERIOUS PROBLEM WITH THE WEATHER, PLUS THE ENGINE, HAS STARTED RUNNING A BIT ROUGH. WTH TROUBLE LOOKING AT US WE'RE GOING TO HAVE TO LAND IN TUCUMCARI, NEW MEXICO, NOT FAR FROM WHERE WE ARE NOW. SO KEEP YOUR SEAT BELTS TIGHT AND YOUR FINGERS CROSSED!"

Then to make things even worse he warned us that we were above high mountain ranges and could possibly have trouble flying blind close to the steep sides of the hills. Even with the surrounding danger he knew that plowing through the clouds to land had to be done.

None of us panicked—not yet. But when the pilot called to the small airport below us he shot a huge surge of fear into me when he said on the radio, "Tucumcari, this is private flight 1307 above you issuing a mayday call. This is mayday, mayday. Please keep your main runway clear."

I knew the word mayday meant big trouble and to add to that warning he said to us, "All of you look for a hole in the clouds. Holler if you see one. We need to get out of these mountains as fast as we can."

Now I started getting nervous as I looked at Seymour and saw fear in his face. With the engine running rough and the danger of flying into the side of a mountain a definite possibility all we could do was hope and pray that we could find a way out of the danger all around us.

As we began flying in circles through the heavy overcast we kept our eyes sharp looking for an opening in the heavy clouds. Then something good finally came our way. Tom spotted a large opening not far from us and shouted loudly, to the pilot, "THERE, OVER THERE! IT'S OPEN! THE CLOUD TO OUR RIGHT IS OPEN!"

As quickly as the pilot could turn the plane he headed for the break Tom had seen. It took only a short flight for him to reach the opening and guide the plane directly into it. Three long minutes or so after entering the clearing we could see the ground rising toward us. Now with a clear view the pilot turned toward the airport and began circling to land. With his steady hand we were brought to safety to the ground where I felt the need to say thanks to whatever force was watching over us.

Following a smooth landing we taxied to the front of the small administration building that had a sign reading, "Welcome to Tucumcari, New Mexico."

I really didn't care where we were. All I wanted now was to feel solid ground under my feet.

As we came to a full stop our pilot cut the struggling engine allowing us to hear the welcomed quiet all around us. Lucky? We must have been.

Fortunate is another word we might have used to describe how we were feeling when the wheels touched the ground.

Now we faced another problem with less danger to worry about: how are we going to make it to Denver in time to go on stage with Jimmy and Doug and do our thing? According to the terminal manager it would take us approximately six hours to drive to Denver, putting us there too late to make the opening of the show.

With the plane in need of repair we had no choice but to leave it at the airport until it could be made fit to fly again. Now we were going to have to find a rental car (if we could find one to rent in this small town) and make the long drive to Denver.

Fortunately, the attendant had a friend in town who ran a small used car lot and would probably lease one of his vehicles to us. We had no choice but to do business with the lot owner. It was our only way out of Tucumcari.

Six and one-half hours after leaving town we arrived in Denver far too late to make the show. On our long drive from New Mexico we had faced another harrowing experience. The fog we had been through in the airplane seemed to have dropped to earth giving us fits to push through the narrow highway. At times we were driving ten miles an hour struggling to see our side of the road.

On Judgment Day, if asked to recall the worst times of my life, I will have to rank high the screwed up trip from Roswell, New Mexico to Denver, Colorado. I beg to the highest order that I shall never again have to live that kind of bizarre day.

CHAPTER SEVENTY-THREE

Christmas 1958

One of the more interesting sides of the business was working with stars we had heard about or seen over the years in movies and televisions. I thought the best and most entertaining person we teamed with was Jonathan Winters. We shared the stage with him at the Tidelands Inn, an upscale supper club in Houston, Texas.

Jonathan was rarely off stage. After the last show of the evening he would often go with the four of us for a late meal somewhere near the club. Without fail he would have a waiter talking to himself while he made helicopter noises or arrow-in-the-chest sounds close to the man's body. Naturally, the four of us were falling to the floor laughing while Jonathan performed.

At breakfast it was a different story. Once when the two of us were having our ham and eggs at one o'clock in the afternoon he asked me where I was from in Kentucky. When I told him I was from a place he'd probably never heard of, a town called Hazard, he replied, "Used to drive a truck through Hazard on my way to deliver a load in Jenkins."

"You're kidding," I responded. "Are you sure it was Hazard?"

"I'm positive," he responded. "I remember because I used to fill up my gas tank at a Standard station close to town."

"Standard station?" I repeated. "That was McAllister's station owned by a family I knew very well."

"I'll be darned," was all I could think of to say.

One evening after our last show two struggling comedians came by to say hello to Jonathan. I'd never heard of either of them but the three comics throwing their jokes around could make the hardest of hearts laugh.

Probably our most enjoyable booking; one week with Jonathan Winters, in Houston, TX.

And laugh I did for at least an hour after all the customers had gone from the club. When the three finally finished their session and the two new comics left, I asked Jonathan who they were and he replied, "They are two darned good comedians and someday you're going to hear from them."

"What are their names?" I asked.

"Don Adams and Bob Newhart. Remember I was the one who told you about those two crazies."

CHAPTER SEVENTY-FOUR

During one of our shows at the Tidelands Inn a mild disturbance broke out at a table close to the stage. One of the four men sitting there was apparently drunk from downing too much booze.

Despite the distraction we kept on singing until the drunk's loud voice began overtaking our volume. We could barely see him to our left as he made his way to the edge of the stage and stopped. "What now?" I thought, glancing sideways toward where he was standing.

No sooner had I asked myself that question and kept on singing did he began a crooked walk directly toward us. Staggering and stumbling, he finally made it to the microphone and in a horrible voice began singing, "You Are My Sunshine" above the song we were trying to finish.

Incidents similar to this one can sometimes make a show very entertaining to the crowd. Seeing four guys trying to finish a song and a drunk doing his best to get in on the act makes for a funny scene.

But to the drunk's friends watching the fiasco nothing about it was very funny. One of them finally came from their table and walked directly to his inebriated buddy. He pulled him away from our small semicircle and began a strong tug to get him back to his seat.

When we finally fought our way to the end of our song and backed away from the twosome I recognized the man who had come on stage to pull his drunken buddy back to their table. Any sports fan would easily know the face of the famous Stan "The Man" Musial. He was brave enough to come on stage and end his drunken friend's disastrous entrance into show business.

In our dressing room, about fifteen minutes after the show a knock came on our door. I answered it and once again saw Stan Musial standing there with a faint smile on his face. He said he had come to apologize for his friend who had gotten out of hand and caused the disturbance.

We thanked him for his concern then asked if he would mind signing an autograph on a menu on the small table. He graciously obliged us and said thanks once more before leaving.

It certainly had been a night to remember. What happened in only two or three minutes wasn't likely to happen again.

But I wouldn't bet on it.

CHAPTER SEVENTY-FIVE

Winter 1958

The following story will be the only one written where there will be no mention of any state, city, or site of a Hilltopper appearance. The setting is rather a swanky nightspot that books only top acts for their clientele's entertainment.

On a cold mid-winter day the four of us were rehearsing a five-piece band for the evening show. The musicians reading our arrangements were exceptional players. Nothing in our book of songs was too difficult for them to read and play.

Time taken to rehearse fifteen songs at this club was far less than what we found at most clubs. As we finished going over all the tunes, the manager of the club came to say hello and invite us to his office to get better acquainted.

He was a neatly dressed man probably in his fifties standing around six-feet tall. His neatly combed hair had the slick Jerry Lewis look that most men wouldn't dare wear. But on him it looked good.

The diamonds on the fingers of both hands looked as large as Hershey Kisses. Anyone trying to compete with his general demeanor would end up with a bruised ego.

"Okay, if you guys have finished rehearsing with the band please follow me to where we can sit and have a beer or whatever," our greeter requested.

Following him through the crowd I couldn't help but notice how well dressed the men and women were. Expensive looking jewelry flashed everywhere.

"By the way, my name is Geno Pascalle and I'm here to make sure you have a good stay at our place," he continued. As we reached his office we went inside and took seats. Geno settled behind a massive desk and continued his introductory talk to us.

"To begin, tell me your names so I can know who I'm talkin' to around the club this week."

Sitting in a semi-circle the four of us took turns giving our names and a few remarks about where we were from. When we finished with our introductions Mr. Pascalle took over the conversation. He began saying that he did the hiring and firing for his club and that he was responsible for booking the best possible acts to entertain his visitors and friends. His final remark to us affirmed that he was indeed the boss of the club where we would be spending one week.

"Please let me end this pleasant get together by saying that if you come to me needing anything and I mean anything, remember that either I or my partners will get it for you. Understand?

"Yes sir, we understand and we thank you for giving us a rundown on how you operate your business," I said as we got up to leave his office. "Looks like you have things in good order."

Beginning Monday evening we were expected to do two shows a night. On Saturday and Sunday we would have three performances, the third one ending around two o'clock in the morning.

About the same time every night a group of five men casually made their way to Mr. Pascalle's office. Each wore a grey felt hat and a dark blue overcoat, giving them the look of New York businessmen. They spoke very little to the patrons they passed. Smiles would surely have shattered their faces.

After our first show on Thursday night I went outside the club to take a short break before our eleven o'clock performance. Already there was Alec Tyner, the band's drummer, relaxing just as I planned to do. Knowing that he had been working in the band for two years I assumed he was familiar with the who and what in the operation of the club.

I walked to where he was standing and after a "howya' doin' began asking questions that I had no answers to. I was probably stepping a tad out of bounds when I asked who the five men were that came into the club around the same time each night and went directly to Pascalle's office.

Before answering he threw a wry smile at me and asked, "You mean you really don't know who they are?"

"No I don't."

"Have you tried guessing who they might be?"

"No, not really."

"Without going into detail on what you asked let me say briefly that they are part of 'the boys'."

"The what?"

"The boys. And that's all I'm going to say about them. I advise you to forget this conversation. You should wait until you're a long way from here before bringing up that subject again. Do you understand what I'm saying?"

"No, not really. But I'll take your advice and for the time being I'm forgetting that I asked anything."

"I think you need to know, Alec, that I grew up in a home where church was a very important part of our lives. I had no idea of what was going on in the world regarding criminals and their ways. So I hope you understand why I sound so dumb."

"One final word," Alec spoke again. "Don't tell your three buddies about our conversation. If you do they might start asking people around the club the same question you asked me. For your protection you should let 'the boys' tag fade from your memory. Understand?"

"I think I do. But 'fade' seems to be too light of a word to use if I try to eliminate something from my brain. I think I'd feel a bit more secure using the phrase 'die from my memory'. Those words have a better sense of total elimination."

"Now you're thinking smart," Alec added. "Just keep on doing what you're doing."

One week after closing our show at Mr. Pascalle's club we were on a long ride from St. Louis to Lincoln, Nebraska. There we were to do one week at Angelo's Supper Club followed the next week with three colleges all in the state of Illinois.

On the long rides from college to college conversation in the car was invariably about whatever sport was in season. Seymour loved the St. Louis

Cardinals baseball team. Jimmy couldn't stand them. I was a Reds man. Doug didn't give a hoot about the Reds or baseball in general. He wouldn't give a nickel to see the seventh game of the World Series.

Doug's favorite sport (which brought "yuck" form the three of us) took place in a rodeo arena. He had been around the sport most of his life in Tulare, California and often bored us stiff describing his days as an active roper.

The three of us knew as much about the rodeo as we did the atomic bomb. They didn't rodeo in Lockport, New York, Jimmy's hometown, Seneca Falls, NY, Seymour's or Hazard, Ky, my birthplace. Our folks liked the traditional sports. However, just as he tolerated hearing our sports stories we listened with limited interest to his exploits riding in rodeos and smelling lots of horse manure.

On the last long ride to our concert at the University of Illinois, I brought up a subject that I'd been wanting to talk about with the other three. I started by asking a question regarding our last engagement at Mr. Geno Pascalle's club.

My first inquiry dealt with five mysterious men who showed up at the club every night of the week. I asked, "Did any of you notice that Mr. Pascalle had company every night around nine o'clock?"

"What kind of company?" Seymour responded curiously. "Are you talking about male or female company?"

"Male."

"So what's so different about having a few men friends? All of us have those."

"Yeah, but these men were different. I was told by a friend that they were known by their colleagues as 'the boys'. Do any of you know what those two words mean?"

"You can't be that naive, Don," Jimmy accused. "Just about everybody in the universe knows that 'the boys' refers to the criminal element in this country. And if you remember, we were told at Pascalle's club that we could get anything we wanted in the place just for the asking. And who would get us what we wanted? 'The boys' of course. That's who."

"You know, I had no idea that the criminals in this country own most of the supper clubs and gambling casinos. I know they're tough people but I can't remember being mistreated in any night spot we worked," I offered. "How'd you know all about this, Jimmy?" I asked, surprised at how much he knew.

"I've known about this bunch of bad guys for a long time. But I never brought up the subject because as remote as it might be I didn't want anyone knowing that I was familiar with their criminal activities."

"So these guys aren't exactly Sunday School teachers are they?" I suggested . "Guess I was just a dummy when it came to knowing anything about those characters. A naïve dummy, now that's about as bad a tag as anybody could have laid on them. I guess I'm in a club of limited knowledge folks when somebody brings up the subject of 'the boys'."

CHAPTER SEVENTY-SIX

March 1959

In singers' personal appearances the question nearly always asked is, "What kind of band is going to be playing behind us?" Many times there is no answer until pre-show rehearsal gets underway.

Along with the terrible orchestra we worked with at a Kentucky college was Jimmy Featherstone and his fifteen far below average horn blowers. They were not a good band. But if you needed someone to travel four hundred miles overnight to play a dance or a show then Jimmy was your man. He wasn't good but he was available.

Once, when we were playing the Orange Festival in Michigan, Jimmy and his band were backing us for only one show. After playing the first three songs Jimmy's ensemble seemed to be worse than when they started. Making a turn toward the band then back to the microphone I said to him, "My man, you're really bad tonight. Keep up the good work."

Smiling widely and nodding his head as if agreeing with me he returned, "Why, thank you Mr. Hilltopper. We're bad but we're cheap."

Jimmy Featherstone's orchestra might not have been in the same class as Stan Keaton's band but he kept trying his best to play his best.

CHAPTER SEVENTY-SEVEN

After finishing a session in April 1959, we went back to our hotel where I found a long distance call from Maxine waiting to be returned. She was due to deliver our third child sometime within the next few days and I surmised by the call that the next few days were close to being here. When I returned her call she said that her doctor estimated that the child's arrival should be within the next twenty-four hours.

With no more business to attend to in Hollywood, I made a quick reservation on American Airlines to fly to Louisville, change planes and arrive in Owensboro around 7:00 P.M.

Maxine's dad met me at the airport and gave me an update on what was happening at the hospital. "The doctor said the baby should be here within the next hour so we have to get our butts in gear and get there before it's too late."

We got there all right. He must have done seventy-five miles an hour going through town and on to the hospital. Valet parking helped our cause. With the main parking lot full we could have spent a lot of time looking for someone to vacate their space.

We finally made it to the waiting room and settled in for whatever time it would take to greet the newborn. Finally, at 8:00 P.M. Lisa Gail McGuire stuck her little head out into the world and started day number one in her life. Mother Maxine was doing great but I had a tough time settling down. From Hollywood to Louisville to Owensboro to the hospital— it was no wonder that my motor was running in high gear.

It was great to be back home with my four best buddies. Cindy, now four years old and Kreis, two, were waiting in the hospital lobby for the word that would tell them if they had a brother or sister. It really didn't matter to them which sex the baby was. Like all of us they were happy to have a healthy young lady joining our family.

CHAPTER SEVENTY-EIGHT

Great Falls, Montana, is a long way from everything. It's beautiful country where the deer and the antelope really play and where the winter will freeze your britches.

We were booked to play a club located in the town's best hotel. Never having been there, we were curious about the size of the band and the amount of room on the stage. It took only one glance to see that the stage was smaller than tiny and that only a three-piece band would be playing behind us. It wasn't the best setup we'd ever seen.

However, we had to remember that some of our best shows were accompanied by small bands more than able to keep our performances alive. Small didn't necessarily mean bad.

Monday night crowds at nightclubs were usually much smaller than the other nights of the week. Tonight was no exception. The only customers sitting in the rear of the room were a man and a woman who had been screaming at each other loud enough to be a problem for the management.

We had just finished the show and Jimmy and I were on our way to the lobby to meet some autograph hunters. Suddenly the drunk got up from his chair and began throwing nasty remarks at Doug as he passed by the man's table. The two had never met but for whatever reason Doug had become the target of the unruly man's uncomplimentary remarks.

"Who do you think you are little fart?" the drunk began his insulting attack. "Just because you're wearin' that ten dollar tuxedo you think you're hot stuff?"

Doug kept walking and ignoring his attacker.

"Hey you, I'm talking to you big shot," the drunk said as he left his chair and began following Doug into the lobby. "You'd better start listening to me or I'll bust a big hole in your head."

Doug stopped, walked back to the heckler and in a composed voice said, "Listen loudmouth, you're causin' all the problem here. So why don't you cool it and go back to your girlfriend. And by the way, if you're thinkin' of doin' some bustin' why don't we go outside and see just how tough you really are?"

All talk ended when the provoker came at Doug and began pushing him toward and then through the main entrance door. I was watching the scuffle from the front steps when Jimmy stopped beside me and said, "I'd better be goin' out there with Doug. There's no tellin' what that ignorant drunk might do to him."

Doug was holding his own as Jimmy followed the two to a grassy spot only a few feet from the hotel entrance. Then without warning the drunk hit Doug with a sneaky sucker punch squarely on his mouth.

The two kept pushing and grabbing each other until Jimmy, six-foot-three-two-hundred-thirty pounds, came between the two and did some pushing of his own. The drunk backed away, faked a punch after which Jimmy sent a left cross to the cheek of the troublemaker. Startled, the confused man made a fast rush at Jimmy only to be met with another smash to his face.

That did it. The fight was over as the instigator turned and staggered back toward the lobby and on to his girlfriend. Doug's swollen lip probably made it impossible for him to play his trumpet in the second show of the night. He thanked Jimmy for his help then went to his room to change clothes for the next performance.

CHAPTER SEVENTY-NINE

When Doug got out of bed the next morning he looked in his mirror and saw a lump on his lower lip the size of a small grape. Regardless of how long he held a cool washcloth to his mouth, the swelling and pain wouldn't go away. Realizing the extent of his injury, he knew that his trumpet playing on our show would have to be put on hold.

At one o'clock in the afternoon Doug went to breakfast in the hotel dining room. The area was empty except for one man at the cash register apparently paying for his meal. Doug didn't notice him at first but after a quick glance realized he was looking at the drunk who fattened his lip the night before. His first inclination was to drop his head to keep from making eye contact with the one who caused so much trouble.

In an unexpected move, the well-dressed man turned from the register area and began walking toward Doug. One of his eyes was black. Below it was a bandaged cheek. Both very noticeable appearance changers were compliments of Jimmy Sacca's two punches to his face.

"What now?" Doug wondered as the man approached him. "Are we going to go at it again right here in the dining room?"

His question would be answered shortly as last night's opponent reached Doug's table and became the initiator of the conversation.

"Uh, good morning Doug," the man uttered softly. "I got your name from the desk clerk hoping to catch you before I left town."

Doug kept silent.

"I want to say how sorry I am for being an out of control drunk last night. It happens when the scotch gets the best of me."

Doug finally looked up from his eggs, barely smiled and replied, "You were a big pain in the you know where last night but now you look like you might be a decent human being. Anyway, your apology is accepted and because it is why don't you take a seat and have a cup of coffee. While you're at it you might tell me your name and something about yourself."

"My name is Clarence Oliver and I'm from Kansas City," Clarence offered as he took a seat. "I'm here on business trying to buy land close to town for my company. If I can find what I'm looking for I'll be moving this way to start construction on a new four story motel."

"You said 'my' company. Whom are you referring to when you say 'my'?"

"Me."

"Me? Are you saying you own the company and that you might be living and working here in Great Falls?"

"Yes to both questions," Clarence replied. "And the very embarrassed sober woman you saw with me last night will be coming too."

"Girlfriend?"

"Wife."

"Boy, she must have had a tizzy watching you make a complete fool of yourself."

"She did and I apologized to her, too. Any by the way, as I was sobering up last night I peaked in on your final show for a minute or two. You guys are pretty darned good. Maybe the next time I meet up with you I'll be able to catch a full performance."

"Yeah, well, if you show up please make sure the booze stays in the bottle. Okay?"

"Promise. Maybe I'll see the Hilltoppers somewhere down the road."

CHAPTER EIGHTY

By the late fifties Rock n' Roll had pretty well taken over the music market. What started nearly ten years earlier had grown into a music form that much of the adult population in America couldn't take.

Singers dating back to the 1940s struggled to sell enough records to stay in the music business. Singing groups similar to ours began dying professionally. The Mills Brothers, The Four Aces, The Four Lads, The Ames Brothers and several other quartets weren't selling any appreciable number of records.

Supper clubs that once offered a fine dinner, dancing on a small dance floor and featuring big band music were beginning to close all over the country. Young people couldn't be entirely blamed for the failings in our society, but their rebellions against our music, our traditional values and even our country birthed American flag and draft card burnings from New Hampshire to Los Angeles.

So what could our generation of old popular music do to halt Rock n' Roll's ever growing popularity? Nothing. It was here and we were to take it or shut our collective ear to the deafening music from ten guitars.

The end of the fifties decade found us and other groups struggling to sell records in big numbers. Going from selling one million copies to ten thousand gave us an ominous notice that the death knell for music as we knew it was on its way to our generation.

"So rest in peace old melodies," I thought with a touch of nostalgia. "Maybe someday the music we sang, listened to, danced to and loved will make a comeback with some future generation. Maybe they'll play an antique record and say," hey, this old 'Stardust' recording is pretty darn good. "

CHAPTER EIGHTY-ONE

Summer 1959

At the University of Missouri we had a great audience at our concert held in the school's basketball fieldhouse. The show ended around eleven o'clock in the evening with us trying to decide whether to spend the night there or drive to Kansas City.

We decided to hit the trail and head for the big city. It would be an approximate two-hour drive, putting us in KC around two o'clock in the morning. We rode and passed the time by talking about various and sundry things such as the baseball pennant race, the upcoming football season and our job next week at Eddie's fine supper club.

Once inside the city limits we followed the signs that would take us to downtown KC and ultimately to our hotel. When we were nearly to the center of town a police car with a red flashing light pulled close to our backside and turned on the siren at low volume. Jimmy, driving at the time, turned to us and asked, "What the heck's going on here? Wonder why they're stopping us?"

Of course none of us could answer his questions. We had no idea why we were being flagged by the local lawmen. So to respond to the trailing police car, Jimmy slowly eased to the curb and sat waiting for the policeman to come and tell us what the heck was going on.

The two officers who had been following us made their move toward our car with hands on their holstered pistols. We could see that for some reason they were being extra cautious approaching us from behind.

Curiously we sat waiting for what was to come next when suddenly one of the officers pecked on the driver side window and said loudly, "All of you get out and put your hands on top of the car. Move right now and don't try any funny stuff."

Jimmy rolled down the window and asked, "Officer, what the heck is going on here? Why'd you stop us?"

"You know why we stopped you so don't act like you don't," one of the officers said.

Jimmy, confused, followed the officers' demands by getting out of the car and putting his hands where he had been told to put them. He then began trying to explain to the officers why they had made a mistake stopping us.

"I promise you sir that we don't have the slightest idea why we're standing here like this. Tell us something that we don't know."

"Okay, since you're acting so dumb let me remind you that your car was part of a bank robbery in Louisville yesterday afternoon. It was your Fleetwood Cadillac with the Kentucky license plates that was seen flying away from the law. So now that we've stopped your running we're placing you under arrest as of this minute."

"Now hold on officer," Jimmy requested. "You're wrong about all this and we can prove that you are. Let me show you our contract with Eddie's Supper Club for a week's engagement. You've probably never heard of us but we're called The Hilltoppers and we're a singing group scheduled to appear at Eddie's beginning tomorrow night. Come on now, look at our contract."

The officers allowed Jimmy to take his hands off the top of the car and walk to the area in back of the trunk. There he took the key, opened the lock and took out his suitcase with the contract inside. Jimmy fumbled slightly opening the baggage but finally succeeded in taking the papers and handing it to the closest lawman.

Still suspicious about our group, he looked over the contract thoroughly then handed it back to Jimmy.

"All right, so you aren't the gang we were told to watch for. But you have to understand that your car is identical to the one used to steal a bunch of money yesterday. So take my apology and enjoy your stay at Eddie's."

A bunch of deep breaths were taken by all four of us. All we needed to have happen on this weird night was to be arrested and taken to some stinking jail. The week ahead was going to feel much better now that we convinced the cops that we weren't a bunch of thugs. We had been called a lot of names in our travels but so far "jailbirds" wasn't one of them.

CHAPTER EIGHTY-TWO

One night in the Spring of 1960 we faced the unenviable task of driving overnight from Louisville, Kentucky to Kansas City, Missouri. We were scheduled to sing that evening with fifteen or more artists for the National Coin Machine Operators of America big wigs, the very important jukebox people.

Jimmy was first to begin the driving duties at ten o'clock when everybody was wide awake. Then came the one o'clock shift and with it the beginning of the drowsy period of the night. Finally it was Death Valley time and my turn to do the four A.M. tour of duty. On this shift I was trying my best to complete the three hour drive without falling to sleep at the wheel.

Halfway through the trip the sun was very weakly beginning to make its move. I was driving three zombies who were dead to the world in deep sleep in the front and back seats. Suddenly I noticed that our gas tank was nearing the empty mark and I hadn't seen an open station for the last thirty miles.

I could foresee a panic situation raising its ugly head. We had to find an open station soon or plan to sit under some Gulf sign waiting for the station owner to open his doors.

I woke Jimmy, Seymour and Doug and gave them a brief rundown of our situation. Doug, who was a shark at fooling with cars made a suggestion that I hadn't come close to thinking about.

"Pull over to the next station you see whether it's open or not," he began. "We're going to start draining hoses connected to the station's pumps. We might not get very much at a time but after a few stops we'll have enough gas to get us to an open service station."

"Brilliant! Why hadn't I thought of that?"

So began an hour of stop and drain, stop and drain until we had collected about one eighth of a tank.

We must have made at least a dozen stops before being satisfied that we had enough gas to keep us moving. Finally, just before the sun got high we saw the lights of a Phillips service station throwing out a welcome beam toward us. Man o' man, I don't think I'd ever seen a more welcomed sight in all the miles we'd driven over the years.

With a full tank and relieved minds we made our way to the Muhlbach Hotel in Kansas City. There we checked in and hit the sheets for a few hours before going on stage to entertain the convention folks.

With us on the program that evening were at least ten soloists including Tony Bennett, Vic Damone, Vince Martino, Eddie Arnold, Eydie Gorme' and other big names from the music business.

When we were dressed in our fancy tuxedos singing our songs in front of a huge crowd I doubt if anyone in the room would ever suspect that only a few hours earlier we were stealing gas like bandits one drop at a time.

Hey! That's show biz!

CHAPTER EIGHTY-THREE

In 1959 and 1960 one of the biggest paydays for groups like ours was in army officer's clubs in Europe and the Far East. These gathering places were allowed to put slot machines in their buildings with the understanding that no profit could be shown from any of them. With income from the machines army officials were free to dispose of the profit by booking performers from the states to play five or six nights a week.

So off we went to Germany first, then to France and England, racing from job to job just as we had done in the states.

One Christmas Eve in Germany, when we were returning to our hotel from a show in southern France, we passed a small town with red and green lights glowing in the streets and homes. At that moment the four of us were reminded that we were miles and miles from home missing the Christmas season with our families.

In my melancholy mood I told our bus driver to pull over at then next whiskey store he saw. Keeping his eye out for a bar or store, it wasn't long before he spotted one and stopped to let me go inside to buy enough booze to put us in la la land.

Normally none of us drank. But on this special night away from home we were going to get totally soused. We did and the next morning our headaches reminded us that we did.

Between foreign appearances we continued to do one-nighters and club dates around the USA. But with no hit record going for us at the time our income from bookings had dropped considerably. We were still making a good living but much less than what we brought in during our first years in the business.

During one of our American bookings word came from our agent that a tour of the Far East had been set for us beginning in June 1960. This jaunt halfway around the world was going to take six weeks to complete. That meant that our wives were going to have to run the households again without our help. They were adept at doing this because of the amount of practice we had given them by being away from home so much.

Manila in the Philippine Islands was our first job on the Far East tour. We soon found that the people of this town and country loved Americans. This affection was left over from the times when military aid from the United States freed them from Japanese rule. We did our nightly shows in the huge Araneta Coliseum, where we sang and received an unbelievable amount of applause during and after each song. "Till Then" had been a huge hit in the islands. When we sang it the applause seemed to get louder with each chord change. This concert audience was one of the better ones we had ever appeared before.

CHAPTER EIGHTY-FOUR

Next on the tour was Japan beginning with Tokyo. Crossing the Sea of Japan, the plane lost an engine not long after leaving Manila. Looking at the propeller standing still I kept thinking, "I don't want to end it all going down in foreign water. If it's going to happen let it be closer to home." But it didn't happen and we arrived in Tokyo on time. Now we had to wait for our Japanese agent to come and escort us to our hotel.

Instead of working the military officers' club right away we were booked into a very upscale night club appropriately named the New Japan Club. The band was terrific, the crowd receptive to our appearance and the hostesses innocently obliging to single men wanting company at their tables.

The week after our successful run at the night club we began traveling like crazy, covering military bases and their officers' clubs. As usual, the crowds responded to the show like no civilian audience would. There were times when we stayed on stage for one and one-half hours doing songs that possibly reminded the officers of home.

During our third week in Tokyo I received a letter from my brother asking some pertinent questions. He was curious to know if I planned to stay with the quartet or was I going to turn in my tuxedo and return to a normal life.

I had told him earlier that the nightclubs and concert halls were cutting back on booking acts like ours and that the Rock N' Roll bands had begun taking the spotlight from us. The overseas tours had become a savior to the Hilltoppers.

In his letter he told me of Harcourt Brace, Inc., a major publisher, looking for someone to work all of Kentucky.

When he first told me he sold books I thought maybe he sold dirty books out of his trunk (not really). He also assured me that his competitors were some of his best friends and that business was influenced very little by political powers in the state.

The company would provide me with a new car, medical insurance, unlimited expense account and three summer months off with pay. According to Bobby, the job was not actually selling books but instead presenting them to committees and individuals with hope that they would "adopt" the product.

It all sounded good. Being at home and having three free months would give me a chance to get reacquainted with Maxine and our three children.

However, before I could make a decision on Bobby's information I had two more jobs to work. After Japan, the next ports of call were Okinawa and Formosa.

CHAPTER EIGHTY-FIVE

During our stay in Okinawa I told Jimmy, Seymour and Doug about Bobby's letter and that I was seriously considering leaving the group. Their response to my news was a short silence. No one spoke until I said, "It's not for sure that I'm quitting but right now I think it might happen."

"If you leave the group when do you think your last day will be?" Seymour asked in a low voice. "Think it'll be soon?"

"Maybe," I returned. "I'll know more when I get back home and talk to Maxine about it. I'm not gone yet but chances are that I'll be leaving pretty soon."

After finishing our work in Okinawa and Formosa we took our first jet ride to Los Angeles with stops in between. Doug's wife, Phyllis, his mom and dad and other relatives met us at the LA airport. It was a Cardoza family reunion.

The remaining three of us scattered to our flights after Jimmy reminded us that we had a date to fill at a resort in Wisconsin in ten days. Ten days. Would that give me enough time to make a final decision regarding leaving the quartet?

Once back home Maxine let me make up my mind without interfering with what I would finally decide to do. She left it entirely up to me.

One day later I called Bobby and asked him to set an interview with Harcourt Brace's Midwest manager. I finally decided that my days as a Hilltopper were over. The job in Wisconsin would definitely be my last.

Although it was a long trip for one person to handle I decided to drive to the job instead of flying. When I finally made it, I checked into the hotel, rested for an hour or so then went to the show site Jimmy had told me about a week earlier.

That night in the dressing room the mood was different from any other night when we were preparing to go on stage. Each of us was aware that things would never be the same after our final song was sung and the applause faded.

Despite our emotional mindsets we made it through two shows in front of a great audience. When I left Jimmy, Seymour and Doug after saying goodbye it hit me that this would be the last time I would see the three of them for who knew how long.

I turned in my tuxedo, suits and sports clothes to Jimmy and then pointed my car and my life back toward Owensboro.

CHAPTER EIGHTY-SIX

My interview with Harcourt Brace's Midwest manager went well. I think he had been primed by my brother to put me on the payroll then hand me a book bag and turn me loose. I believe the only concern the manager had was, "Can this young man leave such a glittering lifestyle and talk about physics or whatever subject to a teacher in Podunk Hollow?" Unlike the entertainment business, a glittering lifestyle in the textbook publishing industry was virtually non-existent.

I was officially hired by Harcourt Brace August 1, 1960 and made my first call on Superintendent Wallace Raymond at the Ryhan County Board Education building. He was a friendly man who talked a mile a minute while chewing Red Man tobacco and spitting the juice into a number three peach can. At one point in the interview I thought, "I don't know if I can handle this job. It's a gazillion light years from what I had been doing in a tuxedo in front of thousands of people." However, I was aware that chewing tobacco on the job was not a common practice among classroom teachers or school system employees. Superintendent Raymond and his peach can didn't stop me from calling on him at least twice every school year.

Following my exit from the music business I sat at home many hours with Maxine watching our three youngsters grow from childhood into responsible adults. Each married and had beautiful children who gave us much joy as we watched them grow from babies into adulthood.

Sometimes, usually late at night, I listen to some of the Hilltoppers' old recordings that take me back so many years. I think about the thousands of miles we traveled together and how hard we drove to get to a college concert in Ames, Iowa or Waco, Texas. For eight years I was a part of a famous show business act all because I loved to sing and got lucky finding the right people willing to record four youngsters who loved the sound of close harmony.

When asked if I missed being in show business I usually say I do miss the excitement of traveling around the world singing hit songs. And even though time has passed since I gave up performing I know that I'll never get all the makeup off.

CHAPTER EIGHTY-SEVEN

Beginning with the simple recording session at Western I vividly recalled the frightening moments when we were on stage at the Ed Sullivan Show. Then came the Chicago Theatre, doing countless one nighters, meeting people we had heard of and admired like Jonathan Winters, Perry Como and so many others.

My memory bank opened in a small mountain town deep in the heart of much maligned Eastern Kentucky. How strange I always thought it was that one day I left Hazard, Kentucky, Seymour departed his hometown, Seneca Fall, New York, Jimmy traveled from Lockport, New York and Billy, a man we had never met, sat waiting for us to come to Bowling Green.

Billy was a shy and lovable man who put notes on paper composing what turned out to be a simple love song called "Trying". The Hilltoppers rode the tune to the biggest and best entertainment venues in this country. Then we kept riding other songs until we put twenty-one of them in Billboard Magazine's Top Forty records in America.

Some have called it fate that we met and in many national polls were chosen as the number one vocal group in this country. I really don't know what to call it, but because of what happened to me and us, I consider myself fortunate to have been a part of it from beginning to end. Sometimes I think that The Hilltoppers becoming stars in the entertainment world was only a dramatic dream, that it really didn't happen. But it did happen and I like to think that any one of our tunes could have been "our song" to couples who fell in love listening to the boys from Western Kentucky State College."

CHAPTER EIGHTY-EIGHT

Whatever Happened to The Hilltoppers?

Following a final breakup in the early 1960s, each of us went our separate ways to Mississippi, Alabama and Kentucky. After taking some time off, Jimmy went to work for Dot Records, opened a delicatessen in Jackson, Mississippi and finally went back on the personal appearance road with a new group backing him.

For years Jimmy had a constant battle with hoarseness. It seemed his condition was worse in the winter when we worked around Chicago and other cities located near large bodies of water. I'm not certain if his problem continued when he worked with his new group. I do know that his condition would improve for a while when he drank a hot mixture of honey and lemon juice.

After travelling and singing with his new group for several years, Jimmy decided to delve into the prospect of starting a booking agency. This change in his life would put him in touch with people who were looking for entertainers to work in various clubs, theatres and other venues.

A very special honor Jimmy received was his induction into the Buffalo, New York's Music Hall of Fame. Since he grew up in Lockport only a few miles from Buffalo this event was undoubtedly one of his proudest awards.

In 1996, another honor came to Jimmy and the other three members of the Hilltoppers. Western Kentucky University installed the group into the prestigious Hall of Distinguished Alumni. Each of us or our representative made brief remarks of gratitude to the attendees.

But the subject of Jimmy's talk dealt with the how and why he came to the University. He used the word fate as the key factor that brought him to Bowling Green from his hometown. To him his accidental introduction to the town and school had been planned by a higher force.

Jimmy and Ann left Jackson in the early 2000s and moved to Lexington, Kentucky where they could be close to the sons and their families living there. He continued working as a booking agent until failing health forced him to retire from his work.

Jimmy's family gave him their best care until he passed away in July of 2015. So ended the life of a man whose exceptional talent as a singer sold millions of records and took him and The Hilltoppers around the world singing their hit songs.

Billy Vaughn—piano player, song writer, music arranger, saxophonist, artist, musical director of Dot Records, played nine instruments, once recorded a twelve piece band playing all the parts, was the silliest man in the universe, but a music genius.

To talk to this man on the street you would probably doubt if he knew how to tie his shoes. Billy was shy to the point of running away from radio and television interviews. He simply wanted no part of being the center of attention. But what he didn't do socially he made up for it with talent and I mean loads of talent.

Billy really had no interest in being a part of The Hilltoppers. He wanted Jimmy Sacca and three other students at Western Kentucky State College to put two of his songs on tape without him being involved. But when the young man who was supposed to sing the baritone part dropped out of the foursome, Billy reluctantly volunteered to take his place on a temporary basis.

When his song "Trying" eventually became a hit he was stuck with being on national television as a thirty-two year old baldheaded man singing with kids barely old enough to vote. The arrangement to do club dates, one nighters and television lasted for a year or so after which Billy went to work as the musical director for Dot Records.

From that point on every recording coming out of Dot was arranged by Billy Vaughn. That included working with Pat Boone, The Hilltoppers, The Fontaine Sisters and other artists on contract with the company.

Only a short time after leaving The Hilltoppers a major decision by boss Randy Wood changed Billy's life. He gave Billy the go ahead to form a full orchestra and begin recording as soon as possible.

And Billy did exactly what Randy asked him to do .. In the next two years the Billy Vaughn Orchestra sold enough records to become one of the top bands in the country. Then he hit it big. A recording of the song "Melody of Love" was a smash selling close to one million albums. The little man from Bowling Green, Kentucky was on a roll.

This success was only the beginning for the shyest bandleader in the music business. One year after his first big hit he scored again with a twin saxophone rendition of "Sail Along Silver Moon" for which he received the first platinum record ever given in America. The same year he was flown to Europe to receive another platinum for the same song that hit so big in the States.

For almost ten years Billy's outfit was voted the best studio band in the country. A studio band is one that records but makes few or no personal appearances.

And so the little man who came off Fair Street in Bowling Green, Kentucky with no car, no washing machine and seventy-five dollars a week job climbed to the top of his profession. Despite his rise to fame and good fortune, Billy Vaughn never changed. He was the same talented man who sat down one day with pencil and paper and wrote a simple love song called "Trying". From that point on his life was never the same.

Billy and his family had moved to California in 1956 when Randy sold Dot Records to Paramount Pictures for several million dollars. In his late sixties he retired back to Bowling Green but that stay was for only three years. He and wife Smitty missed being around their children who were still in California. After their short stay in Bowling Green they returned to Escondido, California where they spent the rest of their days.

Billy died of cancer in 1991 at the age of seventy-two. I went to his funeral and delivered a eulogy which included a spiritual recitation written for me in his song "To Be Alone". Following the service a reception was held where his friends and band members gathered to reminisce about their association with the man of multiple talents.

I lost a good friend, a man blessed with something special that most musicians would envy. He came from nothing and made something of himself. Those words would be a proper epitaph on his headstone.

Addendum to Billy Vaughn's biography: Sales from Billy's hits plus the success of The Hilltoppers, Pat Boone, The Fontaine Sisters, Tab Hunter, Gayle Storm and several other Dot artists were making Dot Records a cool fortune and a major label.

After six years of overwhelming success Randy Wood had become a recognized power in the recording industry. Important officials pointed him out when he walked into a recording company convention. He had come a long way from Randy's Record Shop and his show wasn't over yet.

Seymour Arnold Spiegelman—one of a kind. At five-feet-six inches tall his height didn't keep him from learning the fine points of arranging various genres of music. He loved classical music, pop, country and western and showed his versatility when he began writing music for stage production.

He knew this work would be a long and tedious project so he used every extra minute he could find to jot down words and music. He created much of his play when traveling with The Hilltoppers from one concert to another.

Seymour, our Jewish tenor, from Seneca Falls, New York, loved sports of all seasons. He made certain that we carried a football and two baseball gloves with us wherever we went. A lefthander, he attempted in jest to look and pitch like Warren Spahn of the Milwaukee Braves.

When we were playing touch football in some motel parking lot he would begin announcing his movements just as real radio announcers would— "But no, it's Spiegelman shaking off tacklers as he looks for his receivers! He spots McGuire, fades back and throws a dart of a pass to him! McGuire's on his way to the end zone after a crafty run! And there stands Spiegelman screaming—'THERE'S ANOTHER TOUCHDOWN THROWN BY SPIEGELMAN, THE NEW YORK FLASH!!'"

Of course in Seymour's announcing, McGuire got no credit for busting his butt to get the ball into the end zone. Spiegelman, as planned, got all the credit.

Seymour had a wonderful sense of humor although he could sometimes go too far with his kidding. When he did this I would usually scream,

"SHUT UP SYEMOUR, YOU'RE DRIVING ME CRAZY!" to which he would reply, "You ain't got too far to go ol' buddy."

Having been a music major, he delighted in helping me learn in depth about music theory. All his instruction came in the backseat of our car as we traveled around the country. Augmented, minor, major, diminished, F major 7th all these chords and many more had been strangers to me until Seymour took me to class. He was a patient teacher with intelligence coming out both ears.

When Seymour was off the road he lived in Moulton, Alabama with his wife, Jeanne, and three children. If or when he found time he would often go to the local high school and volunteer his talents to help the student band. But with the demanding schedule of The Hilltoppers he rarely found time to work very long with individual band members hoping to improve their talents.

I don't know of anyone who didn't like Seymour. He was popular with his peers in the classroom at Western and a good student always willing to help anyone who needed to discuss any topic related to music education.

About Seymour's health: through bad genetics he had inherited his mother and father's heart problems and was forced to undergo bypass surgery. His recovery went well with no complications of any significance.

We were together in New York in late 1986 to watch our alma mater's basketball team play UNLV in Madison Square Garden. Seymour seemed healthy enough but his facial coloring had changed from a natural tone to rather ashen gray. I had no idea that his heart was giving him trouble again.

Seymour tried to minimize the fact that he was having another battle with heart disease. But through his surgeon's counsel and advice he finally agreed to undergo bypass surgery again. This time he didn't make it. In the spring of 1987 a lovable man, creative and blessed with an exceptional talent for playing and singing music died in a Long Island hospital. I lost one of the best friends I ever had.

I went to Seymour's funeral with Dr. Bill Ploumis, the strongman who held down the piano's defective soft pedal when we recorded our first song at Western. Bill told me later that as he watched me stand in front of the closed casket he thought about the one in a million chance of Seymour and me coming together and doing what we did in the music business. As for my personal feelings, Seymour's death was one of the worst things I had ever experienced.

My final thoughts toward him were and still are, "Rest in peace my friend. You are remembered."

CHAPTER EIGHTY-NINE

Me—Not the hottest topic in town to talk about but interesting enough to tell what happens when the roving vagabond comes home after the bright lights are turned off.

My last few days with the group in the Far East were frustrating. Here I was ready to head back into civilian life knowing that I was going to have to study to learn what's inside my company's history, math, science, English and foreign language books. When talking to a sharp algebra teacher I knew I had to be knowledgeable about what my textbook could do to help her and her students.

In the Louisville and Jefferson County systems if I could get their very bright English committee to adopt my lit and grammar books the initial order would be $100,000. Gulp! If I said, "He has went home and has came back already" to the committee my textbooks would be pitched into the nearest garbage can.

Fortunately, I was free in the summer which gave me time to get to know our children. I'd been away from them so much while traipsing around the world making music. Now being with them nearly every day they discovered that they actually had a real live father.   Having June, July, and August off my work schedule I played golf at least three times a week with a four handicap. I and two other golfers ran the Lexington Junior Golf program which worked with children from ages ten through sixteen. We taught the basics of golf to the beginners and the more refined skills to the older group. Two of our advanced shooters won the state high school golf championship in the early 1970s.

In fast order: I taught high school and college students in Sunday School classes for a number of years: built a new house on three acres and kept gentle horses in the pastures: went to our son's high school football games every Friday night: helped choose the Kentucky high school All Star basketball team that would compete against Indiana's star players: built a two stall barn by myself and added a 15x25 music room onto our house. I got tired.

Most importantly, our children Cindy, Kreis, and Lisa gave us nine grandchildren and two great grandchildren. Life has been extraordinarily good to Maxine and me and at this point we're still going strong.

A dramatic change in my life came in a span of eight minutes when I scored several goals against a Hoosier High School basketball All Star team. If I hadn't made those shots I doubt if I would have gotten a scholarship to Western Kentucky State College. Of course this would have meant that I would never had met my wife to be or become a member of The Hilltoppers singing group. Was it destiny, fate, luck or what? I really don't know.

As I look back over the years I think of the good fortune that came my way. Never would I have thought I'd snatch life's golden key and be a part of an internationally known vocal group. I've been called a "celebrity of the past". But I've never felt that being some definition of a celebrity made me better than any other human being.

It's been a great journey. I'm glad I made the trip.

Hilltoppers final reunion as special guests at the 1972 Western Kentucky University Homecoming. We sang two songs to the WKU football fans with a two-hundred piece band backing us.

Addendum: Thirty years after leaving the music business I had a chance to be with our former boss Randy Wood who lived in La Jolla, California. We talked for an hour or so in his home then went for lunch at a nearby village restaurant. We reviewed both the good and not so good times Dot Records and The Hilltoppers experienced since the early 1950s. But both agreed that whatever challenges came our way we managed to handle them and go on with our professional obligations.

Near the end of our lunch I couldn't help but remind Randy of the special way he took three college kids and a supper club pianist from zero popularity to the top of the American pop music charts. Then I really reached down into the reservoir of my emotions and said, "Randy, more than any other person in our adult years you changed our lives. And that's saying a lot."

I could tell my words had touched him, but I didn't think they would elicit the response that came back when he said, " Don, that's one of the nicest things I've ever had said to me and I thank you for your kind thought. However, you need to know that if I hadn't met the four of you with that simple little song Dot Records might never have gotten off the ground. So you see the success of the Hilltoppers was the single most important thing that changed MY life."

Powerful words from a megasuccessful man who never forgot those who helped him become one of the recording industry's most influential figures.